Breaking Invisible Chains is a book you read with your heart, and not your head. (I read it twice.) This book is not about evangelistic methods or how to organize a church to reach people. It is a book about saving "the least of these," children living in abject poverty who are hungry for sustenance, who suffer abuse and neglect, and some who become trafficking victims. You will read their stories—told by the children—and they will grip your heart to pray and identify with Al and Susan's compassionate ministry.

– ELMER L. TOWNS
Co-Founder, Liberty University

This book is your invitation to join God where He's working. Intense, heartbreaking, and yet filled with hope, *Breaking Invisible Chains* gives a clear vision of God's power to liberate and transform lives. God has used Dr. Al and Susan Henson mightily for many years. Now their impact has never been greater—read it and see.

– KARL CLAUSON
Pastor at 180 Chicago Church;
Host of *Karl & Crew Mornings*, Moody Radio

Al and Susan Henson have devoted their lives to honoring Jesus by serving the "least of these" all over the world. While many of these stories are heart-wrenching, the testimony of God's power to redeem and restore encourages the reader to both believe and join God in His Gospel mission of "binding up the broken heart" and "setting the captive free." Stirring us to greater faith and challenging us to greater involvement, *Breaking Invisible Chains* inspires the reader in what happens when people move from indifference to involvement in Christ's cause.

— REV. PAUL LAWLER
Christ Church

In *Breaking Invisible Chains*, Dr. Al and Susan Henson bring those who have been hidden by the world out into the light. I have traveled with Al and Susan and witnessed the breaking of the invisible chains. Those that once had no voice can now loudly proclaim, "FREEDOM! The all-powerful God that sees and hears has set me free!" This book will challenge you and, if you allow it, change you.

— SIDNEY ALLEN
Retired, The Boeing Company

ENDORSEMENTS

God has set us on mission to reach the world's most vulnerable people. We have a heart for them because God does. So glad we can be on this mission of rescuing more together!

— TIM TEBOW
Athlete, NY Times Best-Selling Author,
Global Speaker, Entrepreneur

There are few people who have helped Mary Beth and me come to know Jesus better the way that Al and Susan Henson have. We had the privilege of walking closely with them early in my career and our marriage. Our lives have been marked for good by the way they love Jesus and people with a deep passion. This book is evidence of that remarkable love, and I'm so thankful that they've shared these incredible stories of the transformational power of the Gospel as they've witnessed it.

— STEVEN CURTIS CHAPMAN
Grammy Award-Winning Singer-Songwriter,
Record Producer, Actor, Author and Social Activist

Be prepared to weep and be challenged to join in the rescue efforts for the "least of these" and the persecuted church. The stories are filled with heartbreak, yes, but there is also hope. We are so very grateful for Al and Susan Henson and Compassionate Hope for this book and for dedicating their lives in faithful obedience to our Father God. It has been my privilege to be invited by the Father to join Him in rescuing the "least of these" with Compassionate Hope. That privilege has translated into fulfillment of the covenant to being blessed to be a blessing and to make the Lord known.

— DAVID L. DUNKEL
Kforce, Inc., Chairman; C12, LLC, Chairman

As a fellow board member serving Compassionate Hope Foundation and, more importantly, a brother-in-Christ with Al and Susan Henson, it is without reservation that I recommend this book. I have witnessed firsthand the stories of persecution highlighted in *Breaking Invisible Chains* and as I read this book, I am reminded of the hunger for God's Word displayed in the tearful eyes of the persecuted. From those persecuted for Christ in rural villages to the stories of Ning, Elly, and others subjected to human trafficking, and finally to the construction of Villages of Hope, this book underscores the redemptive love and freedom conveyed by the Gospel. I pray this book stirs your heart to action and service for the "least of these."

— JOHN M. DOYLE
Compassionate Hope Foundation, Vice-Chairman

What if persecution wasn't something to be feared or avoided, but rather embraced? That unique perspective is only possible through the lens of faith in Christ, the Savior who invites His followers to share in His suffering that we might also share in His glory (Rom. 8:17). In *Breaking Invisible Chains*, Al and Susan Henson will change the way you see the Church, including all those who suffer for Christ. Your heart will be stirred to pray in new ways and your passion for the Gospel will be inflamed. These are more than just stories; they point us to the story of redemption Jesus is writing in and through His Bride.

— ERIN DAVIS
Author, Blogger, Co-Host of *Grounded*

I could sit and listen to Al and Susan share their God stories all day. I am so excited that the world will now have the opportunity to read and feel the heartbeat of God and the hope this book will bring to our hurting world.

— SHEA GRUNDY

BREAKING
INVISIBLE
CHAINS

DR. AL & SUSAN HENSON

FOUNDERS OF COMPASSIONATE HOPE FOUNDATION

BREAKING INVISIBLE CHAINS

True stories of persecution, trafficking,
and God's transforming HOPE

HIGHERLIFE
PUBLISHING & MARKETING
Oviedo, FL

Breaking Invisible Chains
Published by HigherLife Development Services Inc.
PO Box 623307
Oviedo, Florida 32762
www.ahigherlife.com

ISBN: 978-1-954533-84-4
Ebook ISBN: 978-1-954533-85-1
Library of Congress Control Number: 2022904661

Printed in the United States of America.
10 9 8 7 6 5 4 3 2 1

CONTENTS

PART I: CRY FOR MY SUFFERING BODY

PART II: BREAKING CHAINS RESTORING HOPE

CONCLUSION

CRY
FOR MY
suffering
BODY

THE CRY
THE CALL

y wife Susan and I (Al) have been walking among and serving refugees and the persecuted church for more than forty years. One Easter Sunday while I was acting out the resurrection story of Christ to a small group of non-English-speaking refugees in Nashville, a man stood up and asked, "Did you say that your God died to take away our sins, came back alive, and lives today?" You could tell the Holy Spirit was shining a light into his mind and heart. He never sat down as I explained. Before I could even finish, he interrupted with a public, loud proclamation, "I believe!" Finally, after seven months ... he was the first of what would be many converted Christ-believers! The realization that Christ was a "living, risen Savior" had opened his eyes and heart. His new faith toppled the dead, wooden, hand-carved idol he was raised to believe was god. However, later he told us that it was the love and care extended to his family from the Christian believers that compelled him to listen.

Our body of believers at Lighthouse Ministries fell in love with serving the refugees that God brought to our front door. Many of the children were quickly integrated into the church and began learning English through our Christian school. These new young believers began asking us to pray for their beloved families back in their homeland to come to know their true, living Creator God.

HEART BURN

We joined in their brokenhearted prayers, and several years later I began making trips to their country in Southeast Asia. If I may add, probably one of the best decisions I ever made as a parent was to take one of my children with me whenever possible! Their relatives welcomed us as family because word had spread that I was one of many who had served their extended family and cared for them when they reached America.

As we served these beautiful people, we also knew that this was God's kingdom, not ours. God would build His kingdom through the nationals, not us. God sent us to be their servants. As we shared the Good News, the people grew curious and wanted to know about this God who brought "light" to the eyes of their hearts. Each time before we left, we asked what we could do for them. We expected to hear "money" because they were all so poor, but instead they said: "Many come and visit, but when you teach our hearts burn within us and we long for more! Please come teach us about this light that burns our soul!"

Their words reminded me of the story after the resurrection when Jesus appeared to two men, as He walked and talked with them along the Emmaus road. Not until He broke the bread and prayed with them did they realize it was Jesus. They almost missed the resurrected Jesus. Then they said to each other:

> Did not our hearts burn within us while he talked to us on the road, while he opened to us the Scriptures? (Luke 24:32)

May all of us have that kind of "heart burn" for Christ and His Word!

When I first started making these trips to Asia, it was too dangerous for us to enter their country. Instead, we raised funds so these "heart burning" believers could cross the border in different safe locations to receive training. But on occasion, we would risk visiting them.

BINOCULAR HEART VIEW

Early one foggy morning, several national Christian leaders and I drove across the border. We traveled the dusty, rural back roads to a remote mountainous village for a secret discipleship training time with some spiritually hungry believers. As we crowded into a small block house tucked away in the jungle, we were welcomed with big smiles. While sitting on the floor, I was humbled by how these believers worshiped God and hung onto every word as I taught. Many had tears streaming down their face. I whispered, "God, they should be teaching me." I stopped and asked how many had been imprisoned for their faith. I was shocked as nearly 80 percent raised their hands. They smiled as if their imprisonment was a badge of honor they wore proudly. I sat there amazed for what seemed like hours, not teaching but listening and learning. With each gripping story of courageous faith in the chains and threats of persecution, I grew more convicted.

As we drove away, my heart and mind were still stirred from the day. I continued to ask more questions as we wound our way back down the curvy mountain road until one national leader spoke up. Pointing, he said, "Just over that ridge is one of the prison camps where some of our brothers are being unjustly held." I knew it was crazy, but I curiously asked if there was any way to see a glimpse of the camp from a safe distance. Looking at each other, assessing the risk, they nodded yes.

Dusk was closing in as we cautiously climbed the densely wooded ridge. I stood behind a tree, peering through binoculars at the camp. I felt as if I was suddenly transported back in time to a scene from a prisoner of war movie that I watched from the Vietnam era. We passed the binoculars back and forth as they translated what we were seeing. Then one man gasped and whispered, "There he is!" They handed the binoculars back to me and pointed. I stood frozen as I watched a dear brother whom I had helped disciple in years past be released from a hot sweat box. He was shackled in chains, wearing nothing but his underwear. His weak legs stumbled as the guards placed him in stocks. The scene jolted me to the core. It was as if I was transfixed in time until whispers startled me awake, saying, "We need to leave, now!" We quickly made it through the dense brush, around the fallen trees, and back to the jeep with our hearts pounding!

HEART CRY FOR HELP

Deep in thought, we each rode in total silence. About twenty minutes down the road, I still could not shake what I had seen. Overwhelmed, I thought I was going to burst inside. I asked my friends if we could stop so I could step out of the jeep for a few minutes. I crawled up the darkening shadowy hillside to be alone and fell with my face to the ground and wept! I was broken. So many things were going through my mind, but I remember clearly asking out loud through my tears, "God, what do I do with all I have heard and seen today? What do I do?" Grief groaned in my soul as words echoed from my mouth as if from God's own broken heart. With tears streaming down my face, these words poured out:

"HELP MY HURTING BODY! HELP MY HURTING, SUFFERING BODY! CRY FOR MY SUFFERING BODY!"

With each phrase, those words flowed louder and louder from the Spirit's groaning deep within. God did not audibly speak, but from the core of my very being I knew God was asking me to go back home to cry out and be His mouthpiece.

I knew He had called me to break the silence about their chains and tell the hidden stories of their suffering to the whole Body of Christ, testifying of the amazing, enduring power of the Gospel of grace!

> Remember those who are in prison, as though in prison with them, and those who are mistreated, since you also are in the body. (Heb. 13:3)

Do you hear Christ crying out, "Remember them!"?

Heart Challenge

There is more global persecution in our time than ever in the history of the church. Dear saints, these are OUR suffering brothers and sisters. We are breaking the silence and releasing God's cry for the voiceless by writing their stories. We plead for others to stand with us for the rights of the destitute and mistreated, to care for the families of the persecuted, and to comfort families of the martyrs (Prov. 31:8–9). They need to know they do not stand alone.

Let us cry out on their behalf before the Lord. Let us be His voice for them in our world. Together, let's break the silence and storm heaven's gates with our prayers against the real enemy who wants to steal, kill, and destroy. Let's heed our Father's plea and help His hurting, suffering body! Don't quickly brush away His tears or silence His voice in how He may be speaking to even you!

May God give us this kind of "heart burn" as we allow their lives and stories to testify and challenge us to deeper courageous faith! May we also learn from them, for persecution is now knocking at our own front doors!

Be still, my friend—find your own quiet place to ponder the hidden life lessons and courageous faith found in Part I of *Breaking Invisible Chains*. Pray, and then go be His voice and retell their stories to others!

*Names, locations, and some details have been changed for protection of those we love and serve.

CHAPTER ONE

UNBOUND
uncontainable
FAITH

UNBOUND

Paul and Silas were bound in chains and thrown into a dungeon, yet their voices of praise to God were unbound, echoing in the darkness. Then the earth shook, prison doors opened, and chains unfastened. This earth-shaking moment released the Good News, unbound the imprisoned heart of the Philippian jailer, and spread the Gospel to his entire household and region (Acts 16:22–34).

Al and I have often said that God has gifted us in witnessing the book of Acts lived out before us as we walk alongside and serve the suffering, persecuted saints. It is like the holy events of Acts unfold before our very eyes through these precious believers. We have seen more of the unexplainable, miraculous works of God displayed among these suffering ones than anywhere we have ever served. Their courageous faith in the midst of such poverty and persecution stirs and challenges us to stronger faith. Probably the most challenging lesson we have personally witnessed is the value that these believers place in the freedom found in the Gospel and the high price they are willing to pay so the Good News can spread to set others free!

Paul encouraged Timothy, saying:

> Think over what I say, for the Lord will give you understanding in everything. Remember Jesus Christ risen from the dead, the offspring of David, as preached in my gospel, for which I am suffering, bound with chains as a criminal. BUT THE WORD OF GOD IS NOT BOUND! Therefore, I endure everything for the sake of the elect that they also may obtain the salvation that is in Christ Jesus with eternal glory. (2 Tim. 2:7–10, emphasis added)

Compassionate Hope has made a promise to our national leaders, pastors, and families that if at any time they are ever placed in prison, we will commit to continue to care for and serve their families until their safe return. Unfortunately, nineteen we have mentored never returned.

We hosted a secret women's retreat for Christian leaders, wives, and widows of persecution. We all sat spellbound as Kam shared their family's salvation story and the years of persecution that followed. A life lesson we discovered was that Kam and her husband were bound to spreading the freedom found in the Gospel more than they were bound by fear.

May their story refresh you in your own chains and challenge you to new-found freedoms in unbound, uncontainable faith!

KAM'S SHAKY FINGER

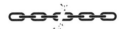

My husband, Gann, and I (Kam) were vendors, selling fabric and clothing so we could care for our five children. My husband would go house-to-house selling products while I managed the shop. While out on his sales route in a rural village, he came to the home of an elderly Christian man. He invited my husband into his house, and for the very first time Gann heard the good news of the Gospel. Gann was so hungry to hear more that he stayed the night with the old man.

> I have come into the world as light, so that whoever believes in me may not remain in darkness. (John 12:46)

Gann came home the next day, called me in privately, and told me what he had heard and experienced. In excitement, he said: "Our family must put our faith in this living God from now on—we must believe in Jesus, just like the people in that village. This is the only way that we can be forgiven of our sins. Our sins have placed us so deep in debt. We have become like slaves. We have no peace. We must trust Jesus so that He can save us from our sins!"

I was in shock, wondering, who was this man in front of me talking such nonsense! Many things were running through my head. I did not believe at first. However, Gann's excitement about this new freedom from his sins was uncontainable as he shared with everyone he met. One day he shared openly in the marketplace. Out of the corner of my eye, I began to watch the stares and hear the whispers, and it scared me! I pulled my husband aside and very sternly proclaimed, "If you do not stop sharing this so-called 'good news,' you are going to be put in jail!" I remember clearly giving him "that look" and shook my pointy finger in his face and boldly said, "And if you do go to jail, I am NOT coming to see you!" You see, fear had consumed me. Fear of losing my husband, fear of raising five kids alone, fear of rejection from my family, fear of persecution, and all that follows. This country has a state-recognized religion and anything else would bring grave consequences ... a price I was not willing to risk!

I'm glad that God and my newly changed husband did not give up on me. Eventually, I too came to trust in Jesus, the living God, and so did our five children. Many in our village became believers too. The numbers grew so rapidly that the local officials and others in the community became fearfully suspicious. Officials began to interrogate and found that we had indeed come to believe in Jesus. My husband was arrested on the charge that he had "coerced" many to follow and believe in Jesus—a foreigner's God.

Cost and Loss

My husband was sentenced to fifteen years in prison just because he was passionate for others to know the freedom that was already bought for them through Jesus. Our children were still very young when their father was locked away. My first thought was, "What am I going to do?" We lost our business, had no land, and no money. We lost everything.

Life was so difficult raising the five children on my own. I was selling everything possible just so we could buy food to keep us alive. There were times when the children were sick, and we didn't have any money to buy medicine. Although I had brothers and sisters nearby, they rejected us and would not lift a hand to help. They wouldn't speak to me because I was a Christian—because I believed in Jesus.

Despairing of Hope

As days slipped by, this led me to despairing, dark thoughts of taking my own life so I could put an end to all the suffering. I felt helpless and alone—with no hope. I didn't have Gann. I would have killed myself had I not begun to hope in God. In Him I found the strength to press on so that I could give my children hope and a future.

> If your law had not been my delight, I would have perished in my affliction. (Psa. 119:92)

God led me to read Psalms 142 and 143 repeatedly for weeks on end. David was just a few miles from where he once had his greatest victory. Now he was being hunted down and found himself all alone in a cave. He had lost everything and everyone he held dear. It was as if David had penned my own story of desperation and over-whelmed, fainting spirit. I cried and poured out my trouble before the Lord with David's words:

> I cry to you, O LORD; I say, "You are my refuge, my portion in the land of the living. Attend to my cry, for I am brought very low! Deliver me from my persecutors, for they are too strong for me! Bring me out of prison, that I may give thanks to your name!" (Psa. 142:5-7a)

One day, I finally realized what brought David out of his imprisoned, chained soul. Psalm 143:6 says, "I stretched out my hands to you; my soul thirsts for you like a parched land."

That day, I unclenched my fists and all I was holding so tightly to save. I simply let go and clung only to Jesus!

Persecuted Faith

Months passed. I didn't know if my husband was dead or alive. I lived every day fearing he was dead until one day a man who was released from the same prison showed up at my door. Gann had led him to know the Lord. Gann told the man to come see me so the Christians here could disciple him. He handed me a tiny scrap of paper. It was Gann's handwriting. His letter was short, but hope swelled up in my heart because I knew my husband was still alive!

The man eventually described some of my husband's torturous brutalities he received. I groaned as we learned he was being kept in chains with no place to relieve himself. He was thrown into a dark pit in the ground for long periods, which later caused him to lose vision in his right eye. He developed severe sores and scabs on his head. His only relief from the painful itch was to break open the hot chili peppers he got from his meals each day and rub them on his head to numb the pain. He eventually suffered memory loss as a result of the many beatings he received to his head.

To this day I do not know how he endured such brutality. There were other believers in prison as well. Later, we heard that some men's hands were chained behind their backs, and they were made to bend down to eat rice from a plate placed on the ground. The soldiers would mock them and kick the plate forward and say, "Eat, you Christian dog!" Guards would keep kicking the plate just out of reach as men crawled forward on their knees until the rice was too dirty to eat. So many horrible, torturous things happened. I shudder just trying to speak about it. I grieved over his sufferings but rejoiced to know he was alive!

However, several notes I received later ended with a plea:

"My dear precious family and praying believers, do not let my troubles shake your confidence and faith in our living gracious God who can set men free, even in prison."

Hidden Truth

After receiving the first letter, I prayed to God to show me a way to encourage my suffering husband. Truth was what got me out of "the pit," so I wanted him to be encouraged by truth in his pit. I gathered a set of clean clothes and made a basket of sticky rice. I called for the believers to gather in my home to pray just as we did every week.

> So Peter was kept in prison, but earnest prayer for him was made to God by the church. (Acts 12:5)

This time they prayed that I could get hidden Scriptures of truth past the guards. I had written Bible verses and sewn them into the hem of Gann's clothes, and hid them in the sticky rice. It was a long way to the prison, but I prayed every kilometer. I held my breath as the prison guard checked the clothes and basket. I knew if the hidden Scriptures were found, then I would be in prison too. The guard called for my husband. I was allowed to stand at the fence as they brought this skeleton figure of a man shackled in chains toward me. I tried not to cry.

When Gann saw me, his humped-over shoulders straightened up. They stopped him about six feet away, and the guard handed him the clothes and basket of rice! We were both told not to speak, but our eyes spoke! I just put my hand over my heart and then kept touching the hem of my shirt, hoping that he would find the secret hidden messages.

Truth Abounded

God's Word tells us that we should be "clothed in righteousness," so for the next fifteen years, I delivered clean clothes filled with hidden truth! Gann quickly put to memory each Bible verse and literally "devoured" the truth. Gann's faith strengthened and truth abounded as he shared his hope with other prisoners. Truth spread, and more chained souls became unbound and free! Uncertain whom he could trust, Gann would encourage new believers being released from prison to go directly to me so they could be refreshed and discipled. Truth that sets people free began to spread to other villages as the released prisoners—now believers—returned to their homes.

Bold Petition

About the seventh year, I went before the authorities and pleaded for the release of my husband. I even wrote a petition for his release for medical treatment. The authorities laughed and mocked me. They told me, "Go petition with your Jesus and have Jesus release your husband. Don't come asking us!"

Others would tell me to move on with my life because my husband was not going to get out of prison alive. I should do myself a favor and find another husband, they said. But I refused to listen. I just told them, "I will wait for my husband. Whether he comes out or dies in prison, we will be with each other again in heaven someday!"

Fire Spreads

About eight years in, I experienced the loss of my home—it was burned to the ground. Everything we had was gone. I cried to God for help. I didn't know where to go with my children. I prayed and felt God telling me to buy a plot of land that became available. It was about one thousand dollars. I didn't have the money, so I prayed and waited. A pastor in America who had discipled and walked among the persecuted Christian believers in our country for many years heard of my plight and sent relief. Only by the grace of God was I able to buy the plot of land. Still, I am just a woman. What can I do? I knew God wanted me to build a house big enough to hold a hundred people to gather for church, but I didn't know how to build a house.

Believers helped, and as soon as the house-church was built, we gathered to worship. People gathered and our numbers grew to two hundred. The fire of the Gospel continued to spread to other villages.

> God makes a home for the lonely; He leads out the prisoners into prosperity. (Psa. 68:6a NASB)

Faith Endured – Faith Released

Words can never describe the agonizing suffering and cruelty my husband endured during those fifteen years in that horrible prison. The hidden truths of God's Word sustained him, and he chose by faith to still believe in his darkest days.

It required great courage, constantly weighing intimidating threats of torture against the promise of release if he would only recant his faith.

The other prisoners saw something different in Gann's unbound soul. Through those fifteen years, hope was received, and hundreds believed in a living, resurrected Jesus who suffered, died, and rose again to set mankind free!

When my husband was released, what a glorious transition he experienced! He emerged from the chains of a dark dungeon prison pit into the joyful arms of his family and the fellowship of faithful, praying saints. He came home to discover many Christian villages praising and worshiping God. What began with just a family had grown to 4,000 believers with a total of 53 churches in different villages. That number has more than tripled now. Praise God who has chosen these broken vessels to be His servants. He also called a simple woman who doesn't know anything to accomplish His will and purpose.

Homes for Exiled Children

This faith journey also impacted my children. My caring daughter knows what it was like to grow up without a father. She and I, along with the support of Compassionate Hope, opened three Homes of Hope for persecuted, exiled, and abandoned children. This is a place they can call home, have a good education, and be discipled in the truth that gives hope for a totally different future. The next generation can now be trained to share the gift of the Good News and someday go to Bible college, a vocational-technical school, or university. Persecution is still very real in our area, and it would not be safe for you to come and visit us. But you can pray, equip, and encourage us in our journey of enduring faith through Compassionate Hope.

May the Lord bless you, my beloved brothers and sisters. Should you find yourself in adversities and lose all hope in your times of trouble, know that God will make a way of escape. When you find yourself all alone, wondering where God is, or without a mate and no one to turn to— embrace the One Who gives hope because He is your hope. Like David in Psalm 143:6, by faith unclench your fists and stretch forth your open hands. Let go and receive! He is your refuge and portion in the land of the living.

May God bless you!

— Kam

CONTAINED OR UNCONTAINABLE?

After our return home from this secret women's retreat, my precious friend Kam's amazing story stayed "contained" in a computer for two years until we found a translator. We realized then that we had unearthed a precious gem, revealing a hidden life lesson crucial to this story.

We discovered that way back in the late 1800s, a brave Moravian missionary was the first to risk his life to bring the Gospel to that unnamed village where Gann first heard the Good News.

However, these very first village believers feared persecution and the potential consequences from local authorities. Therefore, the Gospel was "contained" for more than 100 years! The Gospel was never taken outside the fence of that tiny village until one elderly man dared to welcome a stranger into his home. Gann and his family believed! In contrast, Gann and Kam were not bound by fear and were so radically set free in Christ that their faith was simply uncontainable! They just wanted others to know this living Lord Who could set their souls free too. They understood that Christ had suffered for them, and they willingly risked living sacrificial lives for the sake of others. That sacrificial martyr spirit which animates our dear friends Gann and Kam and those they lead to the Lord, has not departed from them. Their uncontainable spark of faith is still spreading and reaches even you today!

Like Paul and Silas, Gann was physically bound in prison chains, yet his soul was freed by truth. The Word of God was not bound! Gann and Kam, like Paul, endured suffering. However, they did not keep the key of the Good News given to them contained and tucked away. Kam and her husband were bound to spreading the freedom found in Jesus Christ instead of being bound by fear.

Heart Challenge

Y ou and I, Jesus's Church, hold the key to set prisoners free. Yet sometimes we keep Him hidden, contained for ourselves, contained within our church walls while many remain sentenced and chained to a destiny of darkness outside. We must not let busyness, comfort, convenience, or fear hold us back and entangle us by invisible chains.

What is at stake for us? It is the birthright of sons and daughters of God, redeemed by the blood of the Lamb, destined to live in freedom. Believe! Faith breaks chains and sets you free to walk out of the prison house of sin, fear, and bondage into full liberty for your sake and the sake of the kingdom of God.

Ask God with whom you are to share the Good News today—then go do it by faith!

Faith is meant to be uncontainable!

Only let your manner of life be worthy of the gospel of Christ, so that whether I come and see you or am absent, I may hear of you that you are standing firm in one spirit, with one mind striving side by side for the faith of the gospel. (Phil. 1:27)

Please take a moment and pray for the persecuted and exiled believers around the world! Pray for courage and bold uncontainable faith in our own lives—the kind of faith these persecuted believers model for us. Pray for the house parents in our Homes of Hope and for the exiled and abandoned children they love and serve every day.

Let us challenge our own hearts to live like Kam—with unclenched open hands of surrender—and embrace Gann's unbound, uncontainable faith.

TO HEAR MORE ABOUT THE SECRET WOMEN'S RETREAT

www.CompassionateHope.org/reviveourhearts/

CHAPTER TWO

POURED OUT
for the
LORD

POURED OUT

Paul exhorted Timothy, his son in the faith, to stir up the sincere flame of faith within himself. Paul knew that circumstances of life, culture, and people would try to blow out that flame. As Paul passed the baton of faith and ministry on to the next generation, he urged Timothy (and us) to count the cost. In the final chapter of 2 Timothy, Paul says,

> For I am already being poured out as a drink offering, and the time of my departure has come. I have fought the good fight, I have finished the race, I have kept the faith. (2 Tim. 4:6–7)

The following story is a modern-day example of a poured-out servant who lived his life as a drink offering. He kept the faith in the face of much suffering and served others to the very end of his race so they might know his living Lord!

> Blessed are those who are persecuted for righteousness' sake, for theirs is the kingdom of heaven.... Rejoice and be glad, for your reward is great in heaven. (Matt. 5:10, 12a)

Early one morning I (Al) received a heartbreaking phone call from across the sea with news that Gap, our dear brother and "young Timothy" in the faith, was gone! Immediately, I booked a flight to fulfill a promise to my dear friend. I promised to care for his family until they could sustain themselves if something tragic ever happened to him.

Gap was a young man fully given to the Lord and so hungry for others to learn more of his risen Savior. He was a gentle soul with a giving servant's heart who was always smiling. He had been in prison and received beatings many times for sharing his faith while shepherding the churches. He suffered much cruelty at the hands of his persecutors, but he never gave up. Whenever we were in his country, Gap was our driver, protector, and guide. Each time we were stopped at a random roadside checkpoint, he would immediately jump out, paperwork in hand, and move quickly toward the authorities to steer them away from questioning us in the car. Gap loved me like a father. I knew he would have freely laid down his life for me.

Just a few weeks earlier, we had received a concerning request from Gap. He asked for funds to help five families who had been exiled from their homes and village because of their faith in Jesus. He wanted to help relocate them to a safer area, giving them hope of starting over. I wired the funding, the families were relocated, and he delivered the needed supplies. While stopping on his way home to eat a late meal, Gap felt unusual stares and whispers from those in the restaurant. About an hour later, he became very ill and started throwing up blood. He made it to a rural clinic, but his family saw that Gap was failing fast, so he was transferred across the river to a better hospital. It took weeks, but he slowly recovered.

As soon as he gained back some strength, he wanted to check on those five families and take them more supplies. Gap was always thinking of others first. Not making any connection to his last trip, he stopped on his way home at the same little roadside restaurant to eat. Once again, he started bleeding. Gap was immediately rushed across the river. Sadly, due to his already weakened condition, he did not survive. There was never any final investigation (which there never is), but all the Christians in the area felt sure that he was targeted and perhaps poisoned because of helping these exiled Christian families. Gap was a beautiful example of a life poured out for the Gospel's sake. He kept the faith to the very end!

> Even if I am to be poured out as a drink offering upon the sacrificial offering of your faith, I am glad and rejoice with you all. (Phil. 2:17)

GRIEVING WIDOW AND CHILDREN

Three weeks later, inside a modest bamboo hut on stilts, Gap's children surrounded me on the floor as I sat on a little wooden stool, sipping some hot tea. If you visit someone from a long distance, it is customary that you are offered a gift from their home. Gap's wife Pho kept insisting on giving me a gift. I also understood her heart and passion in desiring to express appreciation for how we had loved and served her husband and family. Just to honor her, I responded with a simple request. I asked if the coffee-stained cup I was drinking from was Gap's. Pho said, "Yes, it was his favorite." I asked if I could have his cup as a remembrance of my dear friend. To me, it was a precious reminder of our mutual respect and love for each other as brothers and an amazing life symbol of Christ's invitation to "deny himself and take up the cross and follow me [Jesus]" (Matt. 16:24). I was passionate to go back to America and tell how Gap poured out his life for Christ and the Gospel so others could be set free.

Holding the stained cup in the palm of my hand, I whispered a prayer, "Lord, when I go home, raise up the Body of Christ to be willing to pour back into this cup so I can keep our promise to Gap to help care for his widow and children till they are stable again." As I departed that day, Pho and her almost grown children held on to me, buried their heads in my chest, and wept uncontrollably with tears of thanksgiving. They were overwhelmed because they could not understand why someone from another country, another culture, would care about them. Gap and other brothers we loved had risked their lives many times. I promised them that if any were ever placed in jail or martyred, we would make sure their families were cared for. That day, with the aid of supporters, we helped fulfill that promise to my son in the faith. Gap, like Paul, was a drink offering poured out, finishing his race, and keeping the faith even at the expense of his very life.

> Consider him [Jesus] who endured from sinners such hostility against himself...

Why?

> So that you may not grow weary or faint-hearted. (Heb. 12:3, emphasis added)

EIGHTEEN MARTYRS' CUPS

Nine months later, we were back in the country. Through the "grapevine," I received an important message from Pho asking to see me. I sent word of the dates that our team would be close to her area. When we met, Pho came in the door carrying a cardboard box with the most valuable gift I have ever, ever received. I curiously peered inside the box and saw eighteen unmatched cups and glasses. "Thank you," I said, and we sat down. Through a translator I suddenly understood—and wept—at the priceless treasure inside! In my hands were the favorite drinking cups of eighteen more of my sons in the faith, sons who had been martyred. Widowed Pho, with her own money, had traveled across her country over the last nine months, visiting the wives of martyrs just to encourage them and to collect their husbands' favorite cups. Pho told the wives, "Papa Al has served our families and country and never asked for anything in return. But I finally found something he wants." She said each wife wept on her shoulder as Pho left with a treasured cup in hand.

BLOOD AVENGER

> Rejoice, O ye nations, with his people: for he will avenge the blood of his servants, and will render vengeance on his adversaries, and will be merciful unto his land and his people. (Deut. 32:43 KJV)

That night in my hotel room, I carefully packed my suitcase with these beautiful, priceless treasures. Thinking of the precious martyrs' blood that was shed so others could be set free, I fell to my face! I began to pray and ask God for the impossible and believe that someday He would tear down the walls so God's people could freely worship and serve without any fear of retaliation. However, I also know that God is our Blood Avenger. If He chooses to answer, it will not be because of any outside pressure of the world, but because of the innocent, precious shed blood of the martyrs staining the dusty soil of their land.

The freedom we have to worship today is the result of those who paid a price in the past. That freedom is quickly being taken away. Who knows if someday we may drink from a martyr's cup as well? We all stand to learn much from these servants.

Will you believe and pray for grace, endurance to stand strong, and freedom to worship for our suffering Christian brothers and sisters, our dear friends whom we love?

> Beloved, do not be surprised at the fiery trial when it comes upon you to test you, as though something strange were happening to you. But rejoice insofar as you share Christ's sufferings, that you may also rejoice and be glad when his glory is revealed. (1 Pet. 4:12–13)

MY TEST

In the past, I (Al) had never had trouble getting through customs. However, on my return flight I was connected through a country I had not flown through before. (Lesson learned!) Not expecting any problems, I handed over my passport. The next thing I knew, I was being held under guard with a gun at my head! Why? To this day, I do not know. My bags and phone were searched. The delay was intentional so that I missed my flight. About six hours later, I was released. I was placed in a specific hotel for three days and told not to leave until my next flight. It was one of those times when I knew that God was with me. I was filled with such an indescribable peace inside.

While there in the hotel eating lunch, two college girls sitting at the table next to me engaged in a conversation with me because they wanted to practice their English. I casually asked if they had ever heard of Jesus. One spoke and said, "I barely remember my elderly grandmother praying for me as a little girl for the true God to send someone to tell me about Jesus when I was ready to hear. Are you that one?" That day as I shared, she welcomed Jesus into her heart and life. Now, that answer to a grandmother's prayer was worth my delay!

However, when I went back through security for my flight home, I did think, *If the guards really knew that those eighteen random cups represented the poured-out blood of Christian martyrs, I doubt very seriously I would have been released to fly home.* I still believe there was more going on in the heavenlies than the visible eye could see, because the "real enemy" did not want those eighteen stories of poured-out faith to be told!

> For He will deliver the needy when he cries, the poor also, and him who has no helper. He will spare the poor and needy, And will save the souls of the needy. He will redeem their life from oppression and violence; And precious shall be their blood in His sight. (Psa. 72:12–14 NKJV)

PENNING THEIR "GOD STORIES"

As my wife Susan and I are penning "God stories" of our brothers' and sisters' faith in the face of persecution, we are sitting here looking at several of those martyrs' cups displayed on our bookshelf. One priceless, lone coffee-stained green cup sits on an old, red book called *Foxe's Book of Martyrs*—stories of persecution from many centuries ago. Gap's stained cup is a very real and stinging visual reminder that the persecution and slaughter of Christians is global and is happening right before us in real time today! Revelation 6:11 is being fulfilled:

> And a white robe was given to each of them; and they were told that they were to rest for a little while longer, until the number of their fellow servants and their brothers and sisters who were to be killed even as they had been, was completed also. (NASB)

We are getting closer because truly that number is increasing every day.

Let Gap's life and these verses sink deep into your thoughts as a testimony to the character of a poured-out servant, faithful to the end:

> When the Lamb broke the fifth seal, I saw underneath the altar the souls of those who had been killed because of the word of God, and because of the testimony which they had maintained. (Rev. 6:9 NASB)

> And they overcame him because of the blood of the Lamb and because of the word of their testimony, and they did not love their life even when faced with death. (Rev. 12:11 NASB)

> And calling the crowd to him with his disciples, he said to them, "If anyone would

come after me, let him deny himself and take
up his cross and follow me." (Mark 8:34)

By reading these stories, please know that you are now personally a part of fulfilling that promise to Pho and the other wives whose husbands poured out their lives as a drink offering either in prison or death—the promise that we would never forget their sacrifice. May their stories testify of what it means to live a life fully given and poured out to the Lord for the sake of the Gospel so that others can be set free!

Heart Challenge

As you step with us into the sandals of the persecuted and rescued ones, would you ask God to open your heart, eyes, and hands to what it means to be poured out as a living sacrifice? Ask, "Of what does my life testify?"

Truly, there awaits a crown for those "poured-out ones" whose precious blood was shed!

PRAY FOR OUR SUFFERING BROTHERS AND SISTERS TODAY!

CHAPTER THREE

COURAGEOUS
wife of a
MARTYR

PURIFYING FAITH

The real test of a person's humility and faith is what one does when difficulty comes. In fact,

the persecuted church's number one prayer is not that persecution be removed, but rather that they will faithfully stand strong and not shrink back from sharing the Gospel.

They realize persecution is what catapults the movement of the Gospel forward so hearts can be free.

> We rejoice in our sufferings, knowing that suffering produces endurance, and endurance produces character, and character produces hope. (Rom. 5:3–4)

I know it is hard for our Western minds to conceive, but many of our persecuted brothers and sisters count it an honor that God would choose them to participate in Christ's sufferings. They understand that one of the greatest affirmations of the reality of the Gospel is when one is willing to suffer for their faith.

> To this you were called, because Christ suffered for you, leaving you an example, that you should follow in his steps. (1 Pet. 2:21 NIV)

Suffering purifies our heart's motives for greater gain and glory. Just as grain is sifted before being ground into flour, suffering sifts impurities from our hearts.

> For our light and momentary troubles are achieving for us an eternal glory that far outweighs them all. (2 Cor. 4:17 NIV)

However, pain, loss, and suffering can shake even the strongest believer, especially when the unexpected takes your breath away and challenges your faith. Do we shrink back in fear and doubt, or do we stand and roar like a bold lion?

NARU'S WIDOW

Naru was a man on a mission. He was known as the traveling preacher in his region. He was courageous and did not back down to threats or stop sharing about his Jesus—the One Who could set people free from the bondage of sin and shame and give eternal life. I (Al), along with many others, had mentored and encouraged him for several years. To protect Naru's family, we had to be very wise, so I never personally met his family, nor did they know my name. Naru was always taking risks. Each time we departed, I reminded him of my promise to care for his family if anything were to happen to him. Sadly, I received a call and it was time to keep my promise.

It took me twenty days before I could reach Naru's widow, Em. Her father met us outside his house before we entered and expressed his concern that his daughter had not cried one tear since her husband's death nor eaten in twenty days. "She's just been praying and calling others to pray," he said. Now here we were, walking into a dimly lit house. The small frame of Naru's widow was a mere shadow sitting alone in a corner on the floor. Our translator and several of us who were traveling together slowly crossed the room and knelt on the floor in front of her. I softly said, "Em, I am your husband's friend. I loved Naru dearly as my own son." She looked up into my eyes and began to wail as her head fell into my lap. Twenty days of grief finally poured out in sobs as I comforted her with words her heart could understand even though the sounds were foreign to her ears.

When Em was finally able to find her voice, she said, "I prayed that the one who loved my husband would come, and God answered my prayer!" I expressed in that tender moment that my reason for being there was to fulfill a promise to her husband. I was only an expression of God's love and provision from many to let her know she would never be alone. "Your husband called me Papa Al," I whispered. Finally, a tiny smile spread across her face as she lifted her eyes toward mine. She folded her hands and bowed her head in respect and repeated my name, "Papa Al." A language barrier was broken by love and respect mutually received.

That mutual respect only grew through the years as both of our families embraced each other. My wife Susan and I have received her precious children into our hearts as our own. With great admiration, we have witnessed Em transform into a mighty, courageous warrior. We admiringly nicknamed her "The Bold Lioness!"

Today, as you step into Em's sandals and walk with her in this journey of faith in the face of horrific loss, I pray you will quickly grow to love, respect, and be challenged by her courageous and bold faith-walk. This is her testimony of the Gospel of grace.

EM'S ARRANGED MARRIAGE

Naru became a so-called "believer" because he wanted to marry me. He was not thinking salvation at that time—he just wanted a wife. I did not marry him out of love. I just didn't want to disappoint my dad because he and Naru's father were like brothers. However, love did grow between us, and we had four precious children. God began to work in both of our lives. Naru became a transformed man who loved and served his Lord. He became radically saved like no one I had ever known! The title "Motorbike Evangelist" was given to Naru as he went village to village, spending the night where he could as he shared God's Word.

Threats

Our "real enemy" didn't like what God was doing, so he stirred the authorities. After many threats, they walked into one of our church services, and our children watched as their father was handcuffed and sentenced to three-and-a-half years in prison. This was heartbreaking and scary for my children to be without their dad. God provided for us in his absence, although I didn't understand how at the time. The believers prayed and, by the grace of God, Naru was released after two-and-a-half years because his health began to decline. Although he never talked to me about it, he suffered many humiliating tortures and beatings while imprisoned.

Christmas

Christmas festivals are a great time for spreading the Gospel. Each year, Naru would go village to village, encouraging the believers. He promised to be back on our daughter's birthday so we could celebrate together. I prepared everything to make my daughter's birthday special, but Naru did not come home that night, nor did he call. We celebrated without him, and I tried to help my daughter understand that Daddy was doing his "Father's business!"

The following day, there was still no word. It was unusual for Naru not to call if he was delayed. Many of the churches tried to contact him because they were expecting him to be at their programs. When many attempts to contact Naru failed, they asked if I would come in his stead. I went to the church to represent Naru. The concerned believers prayed, seeking God for safety on Naru's behalf.

Motorbike Found

That night on our way home, we came upon what appeared to be an accident. Local police were present, and a crowd had gathered. We were told that a crime had been committed, that a Christian pastor was murdered. My heart stopped. I was frozen ... thinking, "Could it be Naru?" The police wouldn't let my oldest son see the body, if by chance it was his dad. Instead, he was sent to the police station to identify if the motor bike was his father's.

Our friend, who drove us that night, quickly turned the vehicle toward the police station. We prayed as we made our way there. My heart sank as I saw Naru's motorbike in front of the building, but strangely, there was no damage!

The policeman asked where my husband would have been coming from, and I told him a Christmas program. He also asked what he was wearing when he left home. It was then that the authorities demanded that a close relative other than his wife and children identify the victim. Naru's father came, and as he walked back from the scene looking pale and weeping, we knew the answer! We fell into each other's arms.

Martyr's Death

I was horrified and nearly had a heart attack from the shock of seeing Naru's body! How someone could commit such an atrocious, gruesome, and hateful crime was beyond comprehension! His neck was cut 360 degrees around, and he was nearly decapitated. His head was held on only by his spine. His head had been crushed by a big rock, and his blood was still on it. The murderer stabbed him in the chest many times. There was a stern, intimidating, and threatening message left that began to spread to the Christians: "The tiger that got him will get you!" We knew Naru was martyred intentionally because of his faith in Christ.

To this day, I can't begin to imagine the struggles as he lay there dying, probably concerned more for us than himself. Naru's family was the most important thing to him. As we laid his mangled body in the casket, I offered a prayer that his death would bring glory to God. I cried out that his martyred body would bear fruit for eternity, and that God would raise up bold warriors out of this tragedy to take his place.

This was going to be the first Christian funeral in our region. A pastor friend from America, whom I did not know at that time, sent funds to provide a beautiful casket in place of a plywood box. I knew it was a gift from God to honor Naru, His faithful servant!

At the open grave, my heart broke when our little five-year-old daughter asked where her daddy was. In that moment, how do you explain death to a five-year-old? Sobbing, she screamed, "No, no, I want my daddy!"

> The LORD is near to the brokenhearted and
> saves the crushed in spirit. (Psa. 34:18)

Prayer, Fasting, the Man

Still in shock and wondering how I could ever move forward to care for my family and the churches without Naru made my heart heavy. I prayed, fasted, and waited. My faith grew stronger as my body weakened from lack of food, but I kept hearing God say, "Wait." Late one night in prayer when the children were finally asleep, God reminded me of something Naru had said, and hope grew. I prayed and waited before the Lord.

> For he delivers the needy when he calls,
> the poor and him who has no helper.
> (Psa. 72:12)

A man walked into my father's house on the twentieth day, and I knew God had answered my prayer. When he told me who he was and the promise he came to keep, all that had been stuffed inside me came pouring out in tears. My head fell into his lap, something considered not proper in our strict culture, but I somehow felt safe as if God and my husband were there comforting me. I knew if God could answer my prayer by bringing my husband's nameless mentor, whom I had never met, from across the sea to give me hope, then I was not alone. God's steadfast love was surely going to be with me, my family, and the churches in the future. God was proving to me that He would be a Husband to me, a Father to my children, and a Shepherd to the churches.

> For the Maker is your husband, the LORD of hosts is His name; and the Holy One of Israel is your Redeemer, the God of the whole earth He is called. (Isa. 54:5)

Tiger's Mouth Shut

My husband was the provincial leader for all the Christian churches in our region, that were sanctioned by the government. His death left a gaping hole in leadership and shepherding the flock. The intimidating words, "The tiger that got him will get you," still echoed and caused fear in many of those gathering for church.

During my fasting time and prayer, I felt God urging me to call the churches all together to pray. But I hesitated, thinking, "Who am I? I'm just a woman." As we gathered, I could see hearts still heavy from the loss of their shepherd, Naru. Their faith was chained by fear. Yet, when I stood, a boldness came upon me as I shared the need to pray boldly in faith for unity, direction, and revival fires to spread. I urged them that we must start inside our own circle, humbling ourselves together before God. God's Spirit laid heavy upon us. Many hearts were broken in repentance as God began stirring and moving.

Faith shook off chains of fear as the Gospel went forth! The tiger's mouth was shut, and the lions roared!

Picking Up the Mantle

Most Christians in our rural region were very young believers. Many of the pastors were self-taught and not yet trained in God's Word. There was some concern that false doctrine and "wolves in sheep clothing" could easily slip in without someone like Naru. A committee met and asked if I would consider stepping in to be the provincial leader to help encourage the leadership in the region.

I was very reluctant because I was just an ordinary woman. Why were they asking me? That night I prayed, seeking God's will. In my mind, I was not qualified. Most of what I had learned was from Naru. I wouldn't know what to do. However, I did know in my heart that the church needed unity, guidance, and revival. Torn by many voices, I began to fast, pray, and seek the face of God.

On day fifteen of being in God's presence, the churches and committee gathered. Together again, we cried out to God for unity and revival! As we cried out to God, He moved in our hearts and courage rose! By faith that night I picked up my husband's mantle to encourage and care for the churches and I stepped into God's calling saying, "Here I am Lord. Send me, an ordinary woman."

Fruit in Life and Death

From the day I lost Naru until now, there have been many struggles and difficulties, both in having to raise the children alone and in service to the body of believers. However, I learned in the midst of those struggles to lean on the Lord and trust in His strength. In doing so, we have seen the church grow and expand. Many people have come to salvation in the Lord because of Naru's life and death.

What he had hoped to see in the churches is now being accomplished. Naru wanted to make sure they had faithful, strong pastors and elders who would lead and shepherd the people. God blessed, and we are seeing people come daily to Christ, just as it was written in Scripture. Five of the nine villages in one province have come to Christ and have established a Bible-believing church.

Measured Persecution

In the meantime, persecution has risen because of our real enemy, Satan. The rapid growth has caused opposition, but we are not discouraged. It is amazing to behold because whatever the measure of persecution, that same growth expands in the churches. Believers will not abandon the faith, and we continue to encourage one another with the Word of God and with our testimony of God's faithfulness. We are doing our part to fulfill the Great Commission of Matthew 28.

In some areas, Satan is working hard. Hatred toward Christians is real. What we are fighting is not carnal but spiritual. There is a real war in the heavenlies, battling over souls and territories. For hundreds of centuries, the enemy has reigned, and he is losing ground. We face battles here that you, in America, don't openly face. Generation after generation has participated in ancestral spiritism and animistic worship. If something bad happens to people after becoming Christians, the unbelievers proclaim that Christians have angered their ancestors' spirits. They are right, but really it is demonic spirits!

In one province, many churches are being threatened to be shut down. Just a few months ago—right in the middle of worship—authorities came in and imprisoned the pastors and several leading elders because they refused to shut down. A group gathered in another province, and the authorities locked the whole congregation inside the church with no food or water for four days. Each day they were told that if they did not sign the papers to deny their faith, they would die in the church. The tormenters mocked by saying, "Let's see if God delivers now!" Some who had tiny children eventually signed the papers to save their babies.

After five days, the congregation was put outside and their church was burned. Their homes were confiscated and all their rice and animals were taken. Forced to walk to an open field, they were made to start over with absolutely nothing but the clothes on their backs. No one from outside was allowed to help them; even medical care was denied. At night, Christians secretly began slipping in items to help them survive. Eventually, the congregation was able to rebuild.

Each time persecution hits, I feel their pain and carry their burden. It makes it difficult when our family has a dry, comfortable home, and they are sleeping on the wet ground. It is heartbreaking because we are one body: These are our brothers and sisters! Many are in prison today as I share this story. Please pray for them as they willingly lay down their lives for the cause of Christ. Pray for provision and endurance for their families to stand strong in the face of persecution!

Naru's Killer Forgiven

We later discovered who the man was that martyred Naru. He was never charged with the murder. However, he was fired for misconduct for being with a mistress and was in jail for selling drugs. After he killed Naru, he went straight to one of his relatives and told him: "I just killed your pastor and I will kill you if you don't stop believing in that God you worship. Remember—'The tiger that got him will get you'!" He was filled with demon-like hatred.

God says in Scripture that we are to love our enemies and do good to those who despise and persecute us. So, I went to the jail with another pastor. I wanted the killer to hear the Gospel so he would have a chance to find salvation before he died. His relatives, who are Christians, asked me if I had any bitterness now, knowing that it was their relative who killed my husband. I told them that revenge belongs only to the Lord. I have forgiven all. I have committed everything to God. I will continue to pray for him to receive Jesus before he dies.

Sun's Heart and Home

It was hard at times on my children as they grew up without their father by their side. Thanks to supporters with Compassionate Hope, my oldest son, Sun, was able to live in one of the Homes of Hope where there was strong male leadership and training for those who wanted to serve the Lord in the future. It was there that he also met his beautiful, loving future wife.

Later, he and his wife, Yin, felt that they wanted to go back and serve in the very area where his father was martyred. Together, we all sat and shared that burden with Papa Al and Mom Susan, and we prayed. With their leadership and together with the faithful sponsors and partners of Compassionate Hope, we now have a Home of Hope for children of persecution! What a joy and privilege to serve "the least of these" together. We can only do this because of the faithful givers and home sponsors. We, however, get the incredible privilege to love and train these precious ones to be mighty warriors for their generation.

Thank you, Papa Al and Mom Susan and supporters, for loving and embracing our people as your own family. We were strangers, but you welcomed us into your hearts and lives. You have discipled and trained us. Thank you, partners of Compassionate Hope who pray for us and have given from your own table to help us in building our churches, training centers, and Homes of Hope for children of persecution. We need you! We need to know we are not alone in our battles.

Em's Cry to the American Church

God bless you! I especially thank you for the ministry of prayer for the persecuted church—we are family. We are your brothers and sisters. Jesus said that if anyone is weary or heavy laden, come to Him and He will give you rest (Matt. 11:28). I will rest better knowing that you are praying for us. We face persecution every day, and some believers are in prison right now for their faith. Their families suffer in their absence. Please continue to pray for endurance and stronger faith! We know we cannot do anything apart from prayer.

I pray that you will receive the love that comes from our Father, Who sees hearts and not race. I encourage you in the Western world to have a much deeper, sacrificial love for Jesus. I pray that you be found more faithful and bold in sharing the gift of the Gospel, so that together we bear much fruit where you live and more fruit here in my country.

I guess if I have one regret, it is that when my husband was alive, I didn't see the burden to serve alongside him more. The flame of my heart was comfortable because I relied more on my husband and his faith than on God. God opened my eyes, and I repented.

So I say to all of us, fear and complacency are destroyers of our faith. It changes our focus from God to ourselves; it makes us look inward instead of upward.

An overabundance of fear and complacency can cause us to become self-absorbed instead of Christ-absorbed.

My greatest concern and prayer is not that persecution stops but that the comfort we presently experience may not cause you or me to forget our God and cause us to shrink back!

I pray to God to stir us, His children, across the sea and here! God needs us to be bold warriors—there is a battle to be fought inside and out! We are stronger together! May God bless you and your family today!

Christ's servant,

— *Em*

MIGHTY WARRIORS: DEBORAH AND EM

Em's courageous faith resembles that of Deborah, the brave prophetess and mighty warrior of Judges chapter four. Deborah summoned Barak and reminded him that God had commanded him to gather his men for battle, and that God would deliver Jabin's army into his hands. Barak's faith must have been wavering because he proclaimed that he would go only if Deborah went with him. So she rose up and went. They made it to the battlefield and camped. I almost chuckle reading verse fourteen. Deborah must have awakened really early and stormed into Barak's tent because she boldly proclaimed:

> "Up! For this is the day in which the LORD has given Sisera [captain of Jabin's army] into your hand. Does not the LORD go out before you?" So, Barak went ... (Judg. 4:14, emphasis added)

Yes, God delivered just as He had promised when Deborah bolstered Barak's faith. The battle was already won, but God needed willing, courageous warriors to go by faith, believing that God would do as He said.

Everyone who knows our dear sister Em knows that she is a bold, mighty "lioness" and brave warrior who rises up and calls others to bravely go into battle too! Her bold faith proclaims that God is on our side, no matter the odds.

Heart Challenge

RISE AND ROAR TO THE CALL OF GOD

God used ordinary men and women in the Old and New Testaments to step into leadership positions for which they were not qualified, yet they carried out extraordinary purposes for God's kingdom. God's calling is no different today.

It is when you intimately align your heart with His that you hear His calling, sense His passion, and realize His mission purpose. He will call you, not for yourself but for the world. God longs for the world to know Him. He needs willing servants like Naru, Em, Sun, and YOU to rise up and step into His journey.

Do you hear the LORD calling?

> Up! For this is the day in which the LORD has given [the enemy] into your hand. Does not the LORD go out before you? (Judg. 4:14)

And let it be said that those who heard rose up and went!

It's time to shut the lying tiger's mouth of fear, doubt, and insecurity. Rise up with bold confidence in Christ and roar like a lion!

LEARN HOW EM AND OTHERS PRAY FOR THE PERSECUTED CHURCH:

www.CompassionateHope.org/persecution

CHAPTER FOUR

FAITH
over
FEAR

SEEING THE INVISIBLE BATTLE

> So one night the king of Aram sent a great army with many chariots and horses to surround the city. When the servant of the man of God got up early the next morning and went outside, there were troops, horses, and chariots everywhere. "Oh, sir, what will we do now?" the young man cried to Elisha. "Don't be afraid!" Elisha told him. "For there are more on our side than on theirs!" Then Elisha prayed, "O LORD, open his eyes and let him see!" The LORD opened the young man's eyes, and when he looked up, he saw that the hillside around Elisha was filled with horses and chariots of fire. (2 Kgs. 6:14–17 NLT)

Each story in this chapter involves a struggle of faith over fear, as well as the sovereign protective hand of God at work. Genesis 15:1 says, "After these things the word of the LORD came to Abram in a vision: 'Fear not, Abram, I am your shield; your reward shall be very great.'"

INVISIBLE SHIELD

Sometimes as we walk among the persecuted, suffering saints, we witness the reality of the "unexplainable" sovereign hand and shield of God like nowhere else. I often say, "When desperation and faith collide, there you will behold the power of the Gospel released and witness the miraculous and unexplainable works of God." Susan and I have seen His "unexplainable" sovereign hand and protective shield lived out many times, and we don't take it for granted!

UNEXPLAINABLE

A destructive tornado hit a remote, mountainous tribal village. The decision was made to take supplies to help the people survive, then assess the next steps. I had never been in that remote region before because of severe persecution. However, a few Christian leaders from that village had been in some of our training sessions in the past, and we felt it important to show our support. I still remember the people's hair being so black and shiny that it almost looked blue in the sun, like a raven's feathers.

There was no air-conditioning inside the truck, so I opted to ride in the back. Everything was fine until we saw a sign warning about a guarded checkpoint crossing ahead. The native chatter was, "How are we going to get Papa Al's white face past the checkpoint?" Well, honestly, the road was so dusty that the only thing white about me was behind my glasses! We prayed for an invisible shield over us and went forward in faith. Surprisingly, when we reached the checkpoint, no one was there, so we quickly went on through while giving God a loud praise!

When we arrived at this primitive village, it was like stepping back in time to another century. We were asked to park our vehicle behind one of the homes and were quickly ushered through the back door so as not to be seen. For any of them to be seen with me would have put them in significant danger. As I entered, over one hundred beautiful faces, all squeezed into a tiny room and seated on the floor, greeted me. I was deeply touched by their courageous faith.

We visited, and I was asked to teach. I was amazed at their hunger and anticipation of hearing the truth of God's Holy Word. We delivered the supplies, encouraged the believers, and talked of the next steps needed. Then we headed back down the mountain. When we approached the checkpoint, once again, there were no guards. Our driver curiously asked another man walking through the gate where the guard was. He said, "Oh, a barn caught on fire, and they went to help!" It was God's unexplainable "coincidence" or His invisible sovereign hand. Either way you discern it—God's presence was present!

INVISIBLE

Another night while out ministering, time got away from us. We left our meeting knowing we could possibly hit a random roadside checkpoint because we would arrive in the city way past curfew. Just as we entered the city, we were motioned to pull over to the side by two military vehicles. My dear friend and driver immediately grabbed the registration papers and his documentation. He hurried quickly toward the guard to help divert him from our car.

I was sitting in the back seat praying and another national was sitting up front. We suddenly saw the passenger side door of the military vehicle open. Out stepped a second armed guard who approached our car with his hand on his machine gun. Taking out his flashlight, he motioned to the national in the front seat to roll down the window. He shined the light in his face as he asked a few questions. The guard shined the bright light back and forth across the back seat, but the light never stopped on me, and the guard walked away.

When our driver got in the car and started to drive away both he and the national said in amazement, "How did that guard not see you, Papa Al? It was like you were invisible to him!" We knew God's invisible shield and hand protected us once again and we gave thanks.

When I called my wife Susan the next day, I told her of God's protection. She immediately asked what time that took place and I told her. She said, "You are not going to believe this! At that same time, I felt an urgency to send out emails, texts, Facebook posts, and phone calls to our praying partners. I asked them to pray specifically: 'God, make Al visible to those who are ready to hear the Gospel and make him invisible to those who would want to bring him harm.'" Prayers were being offered up on the other side of the world at the very same time, specifically for a divine invisible shield of protection! I'm also thankful for a praying wife who was "tuned in" to the Holy Spirit's promptings and who is one in life, heart, and ministry with me! This is a real lesson to heed when the Holy Spirit urges you to pray for someone.

In Luke 4:28–30, the crowd was angry with Jesus and was going to throw Him off a cliff, but He walked right through the crowd. They never saw Him as He walked past them and went on His way.

WHEN DARKNESS WALKED IN

Faith is the deliberate choice to believe in the invisible hand of God regardless of your circumstances. It is based on the very character and nature of God.

Our dilemma is we tend to trust God only on the level we know Him. The more we intimately come to know His character and His ways, the more we will choose to trust.

FEAR OR FAITH

I (Susan) have learned that my faith can be fragile. One day I am praying bold prayers of faith, and the next day triggers hit that can overwhelm me with fears and doubts! On a trip into an undisclosed country of suffering saints, God was teaching me that faith is risky, but He is always present in the risk.

The first day, the team witnessed a heartbreaking scene as we walked on the ashes of an entire village: twenty-eight homes and a church that were burned to the ground because of the villagers' faith. The second day, we traveled four hours in the opposite direction to a very rural and poor tribal village facing high persecution. This day presented me with a series of scary tests of risky faith.

Thirty minutes from our destination, we stopped to eat a late lunch. We had already been warned to keep our antennas up because this area had a heavy military influence. After ordering our food, one national leader said, "Let's pray." Hmm, some of us looked around at each other and wondered the same thing: Are we going to pray with our eyes closed and heads bowed, or are we going to pray with our eyes open and act like someone is just talking? He said, "We will not deny God before man. Let's pray." When the "Amen" was said, we looked up. The military policeman at the next table stood up and turned his chair around. He sat down facing us with crossed arms and stern, staring eyes. He was clearly letting us know that we were being watched. We talked quieter and ate faster!

RISKY FAITH

We watched closely when we left the city to make sure we were not being followed. Fifteen minutes out, we crossed an unforeseen obstacle that would have scared me to death on any normal day because I simply don't like heights. Instead, desperation and faith collided! I was sitting by a window in the back of the van when we came to a sudden stop. The foreign chatter by the nationals finally reached me in English.

At first, I swallowed in a big gulp of fear.

The problem ahead of us was a quarter-mile-long wooden bridge that was designed for rice tractors—not big, heavy vans. Secondly, there were absolutely no guard rails. It had one long row of wooden planks on the left, then an open space in the middle, with another long row of wooden planks on the right. So, the dilemma was: Can our driver keep all four tires on those loosely nailed planks all the way across this nearly quarter of a mile makeshift bridge? The steep ravine below was four hundred yards deep and at the bottom lay several vehicles that didn't make it across.

Surprisingly, I was not given the chance to vote or even the option to get out! Next thing I knew, we were backing up and lining up straight with the bridge. In faith I prayed, "Lord, we are Yours, and this is Your mission, not ours; I commit my heart and life into Your hands." Before I even finished those words, the engine revved up and we flew across the bridge on wings of prayers. Fear gave way for faith!

For He will give His angels charge concerning you, to guard you in all your ways.
(Psa. 91:1 NASB)

WHEN DARKNESS WALKED IN

Pulling onto the property of the little house-church, we were quickly met and motioned to pull to the back to help conceal the van. Smiles and some cautious looks greeted us. Some of the children were afraid of Al and me because they had never seen a white face before. These gracious people had sacrificed greatly to prepare a covenant meal to welcome us into their family. We sat on the floor in a circle and the modest home was filled with tender hearts of praise.

After worship and prayer, all the men and area pastors quietly squeezed into a side room. They shut the door to give updates on the level of the persecution and strategize together on the spread of the Good News. I found myself left in the room filled with the echoing chatter of a rural village language I had never heard. How do you engage with women and children with whom you can't communicate? I asked myself, *Do I just sit here like a bump on a log and smile for another hour?* I pulled out my camera and with a few hand motions I asked if I could take some pictures. I took a few shots of the kids and showed their cute faces on the screen, and laughter and giggles filled the room. Suddenly, I had a lot of new friends. Photos and laughter broke a language barrier so that acceptance and love could be embraced.

About forty minutes later, I had a dead battery, so I sat down on the floor and placed the camera in my bag. Pointing out items in the room, I asked the children to teach me how to name them in their language. I would then teach them the English word. They laughed at me a lot as I tried to use their tonal language. I pulled out a coin from my pocket and showed the kids. Then I put both my hands behind my back and quickly brought my two fists in front of me, motioning them to pick the hand with the coin. High fives turned into cheers and suddenly they all wanted to "Find the Coin."

The pastor's wife of the house-church smiled and came and sat next to me as I played with the kids. Out of the corner of my right eye, I noticed a tall, dark figure enter the front door. I didn't remember seeing this man during the meal or worship time. When he entered, a strange darkness walked in with him. He had tousled, dark, greasy hair and was wearing really dirty, torn, and ragged clothes. He came and sat next to the pastor's wife, and they began to talk. She didn't seem concerned, so I kept playing our coin game with the kids, but my fight or flight sensors tuned in. I began to silently pray. A dark heaviness began to wrap around me. I still can't explain what happened next, but suddenly I understood what the strange man and the pastor's wife were talking about. I realized that we were in potential danger!

How I understood a language that I never heard before, I can't explain. Thankfully, when the stranger asked where we were from, the pastor's wife told him Thailand and not the United States. Technically, that is where we first entered Asia. When the stranger walked out of the door, the darkness did not leave; instead, it got heavier. Although I felt cautious, I had an unexplainable peace inside me, even in the midst of the darkness. However, I was very aware that God's presence and shield of protection were there to warn us. I also knew that Al and the leaders were not aware that darkness was lurking outside their door.

ESTHER FAITH

I felt like Queen Esther rising up, tapping on the forbidden door, and waiting to receive permission to enter, because even now in this culture, women are not allowed in meetings with the men.

I tapped lightly. Thankfully, Al was sitting right at the doorway and cracked it open about two inches. Calmly I said, "Honey, there is something you need to be aware of. But first, I just want you to know that I trust you and whatever decision you make—I will stand with you in it." Looking past his confused look, I repeated to him what I saw, felt, and somehow miraculously understood in a language I had never heard before. I added that the stranger was also asking where we were from and that when he left, the darkness and heaviness didn't leave. I concluded, "I feel we could be in potential danger, but I will trust whatever decision you make." Softly pulling the door closed, I sat back down, silently praying a shield of protection and covering over everyone.

The men hurried their meeting and ten minutes later, Al and the leaders emerged. Quickly we said our sweet goodbyes and we were off in the big white van. However, my risky faith adventures were not over. Remember: we still had to cross the long and open wooden bridge, but this time in the dark!

Thirty miles beyond the wooden bridge, our driver received a phone call that startled all of us. We couldn't understand the words, but we could hear the terrified tone and screams on the other end. The call ended abruptly. The phone rang again, and all we could understand were cries. Our driver slowed down and turned off the main road. I looked at Al and asked if we should be scared. We sat silently and waited for a translation. Our immediate concern was that we had put those we just left in danger, but it was actually a pastor in another region being threatened. His bamboo house was being stoned. We, in our Western comfortable homes and churches, have no idea of the price these precious, persecuted warriors face every day and how much they need our prayers of encouragement to know they are not standing alone in living out the Gospel.

Over the phone, the national leaders with us gave instructions to the endangered pastor concerning a safe place for him to escape. We were back on the main road again. We arrived back past curfew but thankfully met no roadside checkpoint. Safely back in our hotel room, we prayed and gave a thankful sigh of relief. I learned several truths on that journey, one being that I have wimpy faith compared to these persecuted believers. That night also taught me that although faith is risky, acting in faith can move you from fear to greater faith in Who God is! One thing we all knew was God's unexplainable, invisible shield and hand protected us so that we could encourage the suffering persecuted saints and have a tiny taste of what they live under every day.

Heart Challenge

Spiritual warfare is real and especially strong in areas where the light of the Gospel has not penetrated. Unless you have walked in these dark places, you may not fully understand how real the warfare is. As the U.S. continues to move further away from God's truth, more and more darkness, evil, and oppression will intrude. We now live in a culture that thinks good is bad and bad is good. Therefore, it is especially important to stand firm and not give room to the powers of darkness (Eph. 6:12).

Please take a moment and pray for our brothers and sisters in Christ who are facing persecution today! Pray for enduring faith and an invisible shield of protection over them and their families. When God urges you to pray—take it seriously. There is a battle going on in the heavenlies, and He might be calling you to engage in that war! Remember that when desperation and faith collide, God's power is released, and the unexplainable, miraculous works of God are revealed.

May God reveal Himself to you today in what you are facing!

**LEARN MORE ABOUT
HOW YOU CAN PRAY:**

www.CompassionateHope.org/persecution

PART II

BREAKING CHAINS
restoring
HOPE

GOD WHO SEES AND REDEEMS

With everlasting love I will have compassion on you, says the LORD, your Redeemer. (Isa. 54:8b)

ach time we step onto the campus of one of Compassionate Hope's fifty-five Homes of Hope and the children come running to greet us with happy squeals, smiles, and hugs, we think of the scene in Matthew 19. Children were crowding in to get to Jesus and the disciples were pushing them back. But Jesus said, "Let the little children come to me and do not hinder them, for to such belongs the kingdom of heaven" (Matt. 19:14).

Walking in the culture of these beautiful children, we discovered hidden chains and plights keeping needy children from ever knowing the tender embrace of Jesus and that real love can exist for them. Poverty, acceptable man-made cultural and religious traditions, generational sins, abandonment, lack of education ... all create a raging riptide that is leaving helpless children caught in its deadly undertow.

In 2010, God showed us that we needed to be more intentional to help as many children as possible get to Jesus. In 2011, Compassionate Hope Foundation and the Homes of Hope were officially established, and today over a thousand rescued children have been embraced as children of our hearts.

In Part II of *Breaking Invisible Chains,* we highlight five stories that testify to the God Who sees, rescues, redeems, and heals the brokenhearted, especially when love, compassion, hope, and the power of the Gospel step in!

These stories are not meant to (perhaps) trigger your own painful past hurts. Rather, we desire to testify to the redeeming, healing grace of God, the power of love, and rejoice in the wonder of Who God is and what He has done. May you see Jesus's beckoning hand through these precious ones, and welcome His call to meet Him in your own story!

God first introduced Himself as El Roi—the God who sees—to Hagar when she was rejected and mistreated by Sarai. While the crowd tried to silence the cries of blind Bartimaeus, Jesus stopped, heard, and healed. When the woman with the issue of blood touched Jesus's cloak in the midst of the crowd—He stopped. This woman was considered ceremonially unclean and isolated from the temple and God's people for fourteen years. Jesus not only healed and declared her clean, but publicly called her daughter! (Mark 5:34)

Through these next five stories of hope, we pray you too will embrace the God Who sees you right where you once were and where you are today.

We pray that Jehovah Rapha—the God Who heals—will bind up your every wound. May your faith grow bolder to be set free to fulfill your God-given purpose and destiny with newfound hope.

— Al & Susan Henson

CHAPTER FIVE

BREAKING *chains of* CHILD BRIDES

They will fight against you but will not overcome you, for I am with you and will rescue you, declares the LORD. (Jer. 1:19 NIV)

THANKFUL HEARTS

Looking back on your own life, can you recall a crossroads event, decision, or circumstance that set you on a new path, for which you now give thanks to God?

One of the great joys that Al and I experience is spending group time with some of our college students and graduates who have grown up through our Homes of Hope (HOH). We have seven different Homes of Hope locations in Northern Thailand. Chiang Rai is our hub city, and it is where most of our HOH kids go for college or vocational-technical (Vo-Tech) training.

Each time Al and I fly in, we send out a group invitation to the college students for a "Check-In Family Dinner." We are met with smiles, a Thai bow, giggling squeals, and hugs as each student or graduate enters. Since our reserved table is growing, we ask a few key questions to give each one a voice to know they are seen and heard.

On one such evening before our dinner prayer, we asked each one to share something they were thankful for. Yeng, who is usually a little shy, spoke first. She said, "When my sister and I were first brought to the Home of Hope in Chiang Kham, it was too far for our parents to come visit. Now that we are in college in Chiang Rai, they are only twenty minutes away, but they never come to see us. You and Papa Al live on the other side of the world, but on every visit you make time to be with us, encourage us, and ask how we are. You see us!"

As her sister finished speaking, Yang, with tears swelling in her eyes, added, "We are so thankful because we know we would not be here if it had not been for you, Compassionate Hope, and the people who fought for us." Every head around the table was nodding in agreement for themselves as well, and then the tissues started circulating to catch all the flowing tears. There was no sense of entitlement, just humble gratitude. Every beautiful face reflected the knowledge that their life would have had a very different outcome had they not come to live in the Homes of Hope, especially Yang and Yeng.

It's estimated that 65 percent of young teen girls trafficked into the Red Light District in Bangkok are from the poor Hmong Hill Tribe, a migrant people group with no country; this is where Yang and Yeng are from. Most education stops at the sixth or ninth grade, and fathers who are looking for jobs for their daughters are easily duped by traffickers into believing a good job is available. Many other girls are taken as child brides and chained to a life of abuse and servitude by an older man.

During the time just prior to our first meeting Yang and Yeng, one of our home leaders came face to face with the desperation of a young child bride. After school one evening, some of the girls in one of the Homes of Hope came crying to housemother Naree. They had heard that their fourteen-year-old friend had been stolen as a child bride. This young girl was so distraught that she took rat poison and was in the hospital dying. The girls begged Naree, "Can we please go pray over her?"

Entering their friend's room, the nurse told them they did not expect her to live through the night. God answered their prayers, and the next day she was improving. Then a phone call shook them when they heard that the man who stole her was on his way back to take her from the hospital! Thankfully, a family member came and got her before the lustful older man arrived.

That very same evening, Naree received another shocking phone call, and this is where Yang and Yeng's story intersected with ours. With a trembling voice, their mom told Naree that an older man was tracking her oldest daughter Yang, to steal her away as his bride.

Just having seen the distraught young girl in the hospital, there was an urgency in everyone's heart. A call for prayer went out to our Compassionate Hope leaders and prayer team. Early the next morning, Naree drove two hours to meet with Yang's parents. She offered them a different option, filled with hope for a different future.

Oh, how we still tremble before God thinking, "What if we had not responded?" These young girls grew to be beautiful, treasured jewels and leaders in that Home of Hope, who love God and us. Their lives changed because many people were fighting for a new life for them.

As you read their stories, you will learn more of the desperate plight of young girls in that region. You will also clearly understand Yang and Yeng's hearts of humble thanksgiving.

IS IT GOING TO BE TODAY?

My name is Yang.

It was a hot, muggy day when my father told my sister Yeng and me to go to the market. Only the crunching gravel beneath our steps broke the silence. I held on to my sister's arm with a death grip, constantly glancing over my shoulder. I fearfully wondered—not "if" I would be stolen—because my culture had already determined that. The real question looming over my every thought was, "Is it going to be today?"

> Rescue the weak and the needy; deliver them
> from the hand of the wicked. (Psa. 82:4)

Child Bride Proposal

I was fifteen years old when this part of my story began to unravel. However, in our Hmong villages a similar story, sadly, is written over and over for many hopeless teen girls.

Each year the Hmong people excitedly gather in Northern Thailand for tribal festival celebrations. People adorn themselves with delicate flowers and come dressed in the brightly colored costumes unique to their tribe. My sister Yeng, age fourteen, and I were filled with excitement to be chosen to dance with the other teenage girls from our village.

The beautifully crafted silver-plated beads that hung from our Hmong native dresses clanged with a rhythmic sound in sync with every motion of our festive tribal dance. However, the highlight of our day turned to terror by nightfall.

A man in his forties with a lustful eye who saw me dance earlier that day came and approached my father. He asked for my hand in marriage. I was barely fifteen years old. I did not know this older man or want to marry him. Besides, he already had two wives. After all, what does love have to do with this decision? Absolutely nothing from my culture's point of view!

My father's thoughts were consumed by the fact that I was one of nine children that he had to try to feed. Education stopped at ninth grade in my village, and my father simply didn't have the money to send me into the city to board somewhere to attend high school. This man, requesting I be his child bride, had a good business and could provide well for me. According to our cultural traditions, he would have to pay a sizable bridal fee and be responsible to help at some level with the family of his new teen wife. My father's last line of thinking was, "If Yang doesn't marry this guy, then when she graduates in two months, I will need to find her a job so she can help provide money to send the younger children to school."

When I realized that my father was strongly considering this man's proposal for me, I began crying and begging my father, saying, "No, Father, please, Father, no, no, no, please no!" He was torn because there was a hidden factor that at fifteen I didn't fully understand. My mom was silent. But her concerned glance met my dad's eyes, and he finally denied the proposal. The man rose and left frustrated, whispering, "I will return!" Many of the tribal customs are not really discussed until they hit your family. When my parents sat me down and explained what the man meant by "I will return," it terrified me, and I collapsed to the ground, wailing in despair!

Even though my father's answer and my plea were clearly "NO," the issue was not over. According to our tribal practice, after the marriage refusal—at any time within the next three months—it was secretly acceptable for the man to sneak in and steal away the young woman he wishes to marry and be with her for seven days. During the seven days, he would try to buy and do special things in hopes to woo her to change her mind. However, now that I am older, I clearly understand what will happen when a forty-year-old man is alone for seven days with a beautiful, teen girl. At the end of that seven-day "trial run," the man returns the girl, and three potential things may occur:

1. If the girl agrees to marry, the man pays a dowry to the father.
2. If the girl becomes pregnant then she must marry the man.
3. If the girl still chooses not to marry, the man pays a fine for having been with her. Either way, she is no longer a virgin, and it will be hard to receive an invitation for marriage and a dowry in the future.

In American culture, you would call that kidnapping and statutory rape. However, most women from our region are considered more like property or a possession and have little human rights or opportunity to make decisions on our own.

The Stalking Hunt

David knew what it was like to be hunted down:

> They attack, they lurk, They watch my steps, As they have waited to take my life. (Psa. 56:6 NASB)

Looking back on this, I realize I really was a child just longing to finish two more months of school so I could at least graduate ninth grade. Every day as I stepped out the doorway of our tiny little home, a home filled with eleven people, I was terrified! I knew this self-centered, arrogant, lustful man was coming for me, but the real question was, "Is it today?"

One afternoon right after school, I saw him watching me, and I knew the hunt was on! My sister and I darted into the crowd of students and ran home. I really did feel like I was being hunted down like an animal. After about the fifth day of seeing him multiple times, I realized he was tracking my moves. I was so terrified that I ran into the house and fell into my mother's arms, crying. I collapsed to the floor at my mother's feet, begging her to figure out a way to hide me! My family gathered around me, and we all wept together! I kept saying, "How can this be OK? If there is a real God, please help!"

> You are my hiding place; You preserve me from trouble; You surround me with songs of deliverance. (Psa. 32:7 NASB)

Hope for Yang

Thankfully, my mother had heard of a home about an hour away in Chiang Kham that received vulnerable, "at risk" children in desperate need. So my mom called and talked to the house mom. Surprisingly, Mom Naree showed up the very next morning at our home and said she came as quickly as she could because she understood my story. She had heard similar stories over and over and wanted to give my family and me a different option. She offered for me to come live in her home where I would be safe, have a caring family, finish high school, and would also be given sponsorship funding for Vo-Tech, university, or Bible college so I could have hope for a real future.

I simply could not get past the terrifying thoughts of being stolen and raped. My mom and I looked at each other through our tears, and we said, "Yes!" I quickly packed my bags, and as much as I loved my family, I had to say my goodbyes.

Hope for Yeng

About four miles down the road, something suddenly hit me right in the chest and I started crying all over again. I cried out, "Stop! We have to go back! We have to go back!" Not making any sense of this, Mom Naree just thought I couldn't leave my family, and I simply had changed my mind. But I said, "No, no, you don't understand! If I am not there that horrible man will just come back and take my fourteen-year-old sister, Yeng, instead! We have to go back, please!" Thankfully, she realized that I was right. She turned around and we went back and talked to Yeng and my parents. Mom Naree gave Yeng the same offer of hope for a better future! Yeng held me so tightly saying over and over, "Thank you! Thank you!" Mom helped Yeng pack quickly and, with more hugs this time, we drove away. As I stared out the window, a sweet, unexplainable peace began to settle over me. Even going toward the unknown, I somehow knew hope was just ahead!

> Sing to the LORD, praise the LORD! For He has delivered the soul of the needy one from the hand of evildoers. (Jer. 20:13 NASB)

BREAKING INVISIBLE CHAINS

Home of Hope

Our new house parents, Papa Inkin and Mom Naree, showered us with love, and we knew we were safe! Because of Papa Al, Mom Susan, and the Compassionate Hope sponsors like the Lawler family and friends, we even had a brand-new beautiful home to live in. Most of all, we were taught to know and trust our great Protector and Provider, Jesus Christ, the resurrected, living God! The resurrected Lord is the great distinction between the religious merit and demerit system carved from the statue of a dead god that I grew up with.

> For He rescued us from the domain of darkness, and transferred us to the kingdom of His beloved Son, in whom we have redemption, the forgiveness of sins. (Col. 1:13–14 NASB)

The light of truth shone into those dark cultural practices we were taught as children, and Christ's love broke through the chains and transformed both of our hearts, minds, and lives.

During the next five years, while living in the Patricia B. Hammonds Home of Hope #1 in Chiang Kham, God stirred our hearts to help lead the worship team and set up small discipleship groups. In these groups, new girls coming in could also be loved and discipled in truth to know their living Lord! That was not all! Our house parents, along with Compassionate Hope, worked endless hours to get our proper legal papers, which our parents were unable to secure, so we could finally go to the university.

Compassionate Hope has promised all its children that, if they work hard and prove themselves, they will find sponsors for Vo-Tech training, university, or Bible college so we can all become self-sustaining and break the cycle of poverty as well.

> But now the LORD my God has given me rest on every side; there is neither adversary nor misfortune. (1 Kgs. 5:4)

I am so thankful for our College Sponsorship Partners who provided us an opportunity we know we would never have had. My sister and I recently graduated from the university

with high honors. We have new careers and a future! We now have an opportunity to break the chains of poverty and can help our family and younger siblings. I look back on that crossroads of life experience and realize very clearly that I could have had a very different, sad life filled with lots of heartache. Now, my sister and I are filled with hope and dreams for a new, amazing future!

— *Yang*

> When the LORD brought back the captive ones of Zion, We were like those who dream. (Psa. 126:1 NASB)

Heart Challenge

One day, a tragic video was sent to us of a girl being "taken for her trial run." She was walking home after school just like Yang had years before. A crowd of students were all around and absolutely no one tried to help her. Some of the schoolboys even laughed as she tirelessly fought and fought until she passed out and was thrown onto a motorcycle by two men.

Susan and I cried out to the Lord that day, begging God to please help us to not only rescue, but to break the chains of generational cultural lies and horrible but accepted practices! We cried, "Lord, please help us train up a new generation of young men who know they are citizens of a new heavenly domain with a new culture, a new mindset of justice and faith!" My friend, pray with us that a courageous generation of young men will be trained and willingly stand against the culture-pulling gravity and stand up for truth for the sake of beautiful young girls like Yang and Yeng— priceless, valuable treasures of great worth—so they, too, can have hope and dream a different future.

If you have ever personally been threatened or pushed to make decisions contrary to truth and your heart, seek out help. You have a voice worthy to be heard.

> So He saved them from the hand of the one who hated them, And redeemed them from the hand of the enemy. (Psa. 106:10 NASB)

FOR MORE INFORMATION

Go to www.CompassionateHope.org/collegesponsorship to learn how you too can join the College Sponsorship Team and give children like Yang and Yeng a different future.

CHAPTER SIX

BREAKING
chains of
ABANDONMENT

NOT ABANDONED

Hagar and her son Ishmael were rejected by Abraham and Sarah, cast out into the wilderness, and left to survive on their own. In that hopeless, desperate moment, fearing her son's death, Hagar wept.

> The angel of God called to Hagar from heaven and said to her, "What troubles you, Hagar? Fear not, for God has heard the voice of the boy where he is...." "Then God opened her eyes and she saw a well of water. (Gen. 21:17b–19a)

Many children around the world wake up hopeless every day from painful experiences from rejection, abandonment, abuse, or being overlooked. These tentacles can leave stinging effects on into adulthood and can disorient them on their journey in life. Undealt with, the emotional scars can even distort God's light in the heart and cause one to wonder if God even cares.

Take heart! Even in our most hopeless moments, we have NOT been abandoned by God. Like Hagar and Ishmael, He hears our desperate cries.

Though my father and my mother abandoned me, the LORD gathers me up. (Psa. 27:10 ISV)

Before we step into the sandals of Rain and little Honey's story, we would like to dig in a little deeper to help us relate and better understand some of their invisible chains and for some readers, perhaps your own.

Let's take a moment and look with a compassionate heart into two key words:

> Rejection: castaway, thrown away, reprobate, unapproved; by implication worthless *(Adapted from Strong's Concordance)*

> Abandonment: deserted, left in straits, left helpless, utterly forsaken, to have left behind, to have left surviving *(Adapted from Thayer's Greek-English Lexicon of the New Testament)*

Have you, my friend, ever felt those hurtful, stinging words? We've all experienced rejection in various levels and stages in life. Perhaps for some, these defining words still carry a heavy weight in your own heart.

If so, do not let them define you! Run to God's Word to reclaim Truth. Your worth and value are based on who you are in Christ, not what others say or even what you believe about yourself. He calls you by His name and that makes you quite valuable!

> For the LORD will not forsake his people; he will not abandon his heritage. (Psa. 94:14)

Looking up these definitions related to rejection and abandonment also stirs up deep, strong feelings in Al and me because we know that most of the children in our Homes of Hope can relate.

We have also found that beyond replacing lies with truth, these children need patient, grace-filled, caring mentors. They need extended arms to walk into their darkness until they feel safe enough to step towards the light to find hope.

As you read Rain and Honey's story, allow it to open your heart. It is not meant to trigger past pain but to give you real hope that God breaks invisible chains and brings healing. Our prayer is that no matter your past, you will allow God to walk with you on your own healing journey.

SMILING TODDLER, RELUCTANT MOM

Bright-eyed, smiling Honey came to the Homes of Hope in Phu Sang, Thailand, as a toddler but also with a hurting teen mom reluctantly in tow. When Al and I first met Rain and Honey and heard Rain's life story, we grieved inside. But our grief was not without hope because we know God can break chains. We began praying, "OK, Lord, a lot needs to be redeemed in both of these needy, young hearts! Lord, please break the generational sins and trauma, especially through little Honey!"

With each visit to the Homes of Hope, we've tried to take intentional time to encourage Honey and Rain, to let them know they are seen and loved! We shake our heads in amazement and say, "Wow—only God could do this miracle!"

> He lifted me out of the slimy pit, out of the mud and mire; he set my feet on a rock and gave me a firm place to stand. (Psalm 40:2 NIV).

CHAINS OF ABANDONMENT

The thunder rumbled and heavy rain fell as the contractions increased with rhythmic force. Within a matter of minutes, at the tender age of fourteen, I was handed my new baby girl. She was given the name "Honey." Precious and innocent, Honey will never know her father, even when he gets out of prison. As I hold Honey in my arms, the storm continues to rage outside, but it does not compare with the storm raging inside my heart.

My name means "rain." I am now twenty-two years old, and this is my story.

My mother was from Burma and was very poor. Before I was born, she heard of opportunities to find work in Chiang Rai, Thailand. Life was not easy in Chiang Rai, and my mom was deceived, tricked, and trafficked. She was forced into prostitution just to survive.

Eventually, she got pregnant with me. I would never know who my father was. Mom didn't want me because I was a reminder of the pain she had faced. So when I was a baby, she gave me to my aging grandmother who lived in a very poor village near the border of Burma and Thailand.

The next ten years of my life with my grandmother would be spent in extreme poverty. We were so poor that I could not go to school. My grandmother didn't have money for a school uniform, shoes, or school supplies. Feelings of being unwanted, unloved, and ostracized became indelible forces in my early life. Every day, the children in the village mocked me with hurtful words: "You have no dad! Your mother does not even want you. You are not loved!" These hurtful words echoed over and over in my thoughts. They confirmed all the terrible things I already believed about myself. Through it all, I became angry and bitter.

About the time I turned ten, my mother married and had a baby boy. After his birth, she decided to come and get me. At first, I was so happy that I could finally say to the village kids, "Yes, I am wanted and loved."

I was wanted all right—but only to be a slave in the home to clean, cook, and take care of the baby. I quickly realized I was nothing more than their "Ma-Bon" (house maid). My stepfather made it clear he did not want me. Our home had no electricity or running water. I would get up at dawn and walk a long distance to the water hole to draw buckets of water to carry back home. I would do my chores quickly because I was finally able to attend school. I was often late because my mother said I could not go until all my chores for that day were done.

At school, I was made fun of and mocked because I was poor. My secondhand uniform was old and arrayed with splotches of black mildew. At times, I did not even have shoes to wear or food to eat at lunch break. I blocked out the hunger pangs and the kids' mocking words because I was glad to be in school.

Chains of Abuse

In Thailand, there are Buddhist celebration festivals with free food, dancing, and games for all ages. There were times when my mother, brother, and stepfather would leave and go to the big festivals. I would beg and cry to go with them. Instead of being allowed to go, my stepfather would beat me and tie my hands with a rope. With anger flowing through his veins, he would drag me down to the bottom of a hill and tie me to a tree in the river. He would leave me there all day till they returned.

My ten-year-old body would shiver in the cold water while my arms and face burned in the hot sun.

While the physical trauma was intense, it didn't compare to the pain I felt in my heart. I felt so broken—so alone. My own mother knew what my stepfather was doing to me and didn't love me enough to protect me. She just left with my baby brother safely tucked in her arms to have a good time. I longed to have her arms wrapped around me. I longed to hear the words, "I love you." But these were just longings, and they were longings never fulfilled. I felt unwanted, unloved, and unprotected. Deep sadness, fear, and insecurity felt normal to me because, at this time in my life, it was all I knew.

On one of the days when my stepfather was angry, he tied me to a tree in the river again. As he jerked the knots tight around my little wrists, thunder rumbled in the distance. The skies grew dark and the wind began to howl, but he just walked off and left me there all alone. There I was, a little girl standing in the rising current of the river. As the rain fell, each drop stung my face and mingled with my tears. The thought flooded my mind: *If I die here, no one would even care.*

When I was twelve years old, my stepfather's anger grew more intense. One evening, in a fit of rage, he severely beat my mom. I experienced a level of fear I had never felt before. Watching a grown man beat a defenseless woman shook me intensely. When it was over, he took my baby brother and left my mom and me for good. At first, I thought this would be a good thing. I thought my mom and I would finally have a life together and she would now have time to love me! But my dreams were quickly shattered.

Since I was not needed to care for the house or my baby brother, I was no longer wanted and was abandoned again! I still remember staring hopelessly out the window on the long bus ride back to my grandmother's house. My mother went back to Chiang Rai to find work and live her life without me. The mocking from the people in the village picked up again, only this time it rang even louder in my head than before. Even though I was only on a third-grade level and was teased for being so far behind, I liked school and was thankful I was able to attend.

Chains of Shame

When I was fourteen years old, a relative got sick, so my grandmother left to go take care of them. She left me alone at the house so I could go to school. After a few days, all the food in the house was gone. I walked to relatives nearby to beg for food. All I got was rotten rice and a lot of whispers. Because I was so hungry, I ate it anyway.

One night, I awoke with my heart pounding. In a state of shock, I realized two men had broken into the house. The edge of a knife was pushed tight against my neck. Afraid to scream or move, I froze as the sharp blade pressed against my skin.

Even in complete darkness, I recognized the voice of the younger man. It was my mother's half-brother. The voice of the older man was a distant relative. Over the next several hours, these two men beat and raped me. The pain was unbearable. They cut my left arm with a sharp knife and said repeatedly in tortuous tones, "If you tell anyone—anyone—then we will come back and kill you!" I believed them. So, I kept silent. It was several days before I could muster the strength to get up and move around. I wrapped my arm with makeshift bandages and wore a long-sleeved shirt to cover my wounds and returned to school. However, silence covered my inner wounds.

A few months later, my grandmother noticed my school uniform getting tighter and my stomach getting bigger. She began to question me. Struggling with overwhelming feelings of shame, I finally broke down and told her. I cried uncontrollably as I unpacked the whole horrid event for the first time. She was so angry. She reported her ex-husband's son to the police and then called my mother to tell her. Instead of my mother feeling sad and protecting me, she called her half-brother and warned him to run away and hide from the police! The feelings of complete loneliness and absolute rejection only intensified deep within my heart.

The next months were extremely difficult, as I had to tell the police every shameful detail of my story. Even when they finally caught the two men and held them in jail, the worst days were still ahead for me. I had to face my attackers and all my family and neighbors in the courtroom. I had to relive every detail over and over in front of everyone as the trial dragged on. I wanted to die! I was drowning in shame. All I could think of was how I wished I had drowned when I was tied up in the river. Then none of this would have happened. There was no love from anyone. I felt no hope for the future. The only thing I had cared about was school. Now, in light of my pregnancy, that too was lost. Finally, word came that the two men were sentenced to prison. While the two men faced justice, I was chained in my own prison. I wished I could die so I could be free of the deep, dark pain. Suicidal thoughts now dominated and tortured me.

Generational Chains Recycled

It was unsafe for me to go back to my own village, so Social Services sent me to a "safe home" to live in until the baby was born. On the stormy night she was born, at first I did not want to care for her. With each cry, it only reminded me of the horrible nightmare I had been through. The people named her Honey, sweet and innocent, but I felt trapped, overwhelmed, and desperate. So, one night I ran away and left the baby behind. I attempted to escape the pain and any reminder of all that had happened. I just wanted to live my own life for myself, which drove me into a deeper cycle of pain as I sought escape through alcohol, boys, and parties. If something didn't happen, I would continue to repeat the same cycle as my mother.

Meanwhile, the "safe home" called my mother, and she came and got Honey. Mom had recently remarried a much younger man who was only nineteen years old. They began searching for me. During this time, I had a very serious motorcycle accident that almost cost me my life. As I was hospitalized, the staff called my mom. She came and got me at the completion of my recovery. They lived in a very tiny, one-room hut with only one bed. This created an odd sleeping arrangement: my mom, my nineteen-year-old stepfather, Honey, and me. My mother was now thirty-seven years old and worked as a janitor. She would get up early in the morning and go to work, leaving me, Honey, and my nineteen-year-old stepfather sleeping in the same bed. My mother saw how her young husband looked at me. She became jealous and kicked me and Honey out of the house.

Honey and I went to a friend's house to live. It wasn't long before I had a new boyfriend. He was from Burma. As our relationship grew, he took Honey and me to meet his family. Because I was so young and had a little baby, they asked many questions and argued with my boyfriend regarding our relationship right in front of me. I was humiliated, and the incident created deep tensions. Once again, I was feeling everyone's rejection. My thought life battered my soul: *What is wrong with me? Why does no one even want to love me?*

I began to realize I was just like my mom. Honey felt like an obstacle to me. I began to believe the lie that Honey was the reason I was not loved. Like my mom, I began to believe that the right decision was to give Honey to a better family so I could find someone to love me. It was in this season of my life that my boyfriend got very angry and beat me up so badly that he broke my arm. This event, as dark as it was, set into motion a series of events that would forever change my life.

Hands of Redemption

When I was in the hospital with my broken arm, someone there heard my story and had compassion on me. She called a Christian woman named Grace, who had a home for women in need in Chiang Mai. The woman told Grace about our situation, and Grace decided to take Honey and me in. I was in such pain and could not care for myself, let alone Honey; so, this was the only option for us.

The people at Grace's home were kind and talked of a living God that I did not understand. There was not much to do in this home, and our room was very small. There was no one there my age. I felt very alone. I still struggled inside and did not want to care for the baby. I just wanted to go back to school. I just wanted to be a kid again. I could not see any hope of a future. Many of the ladies in the home seemed at peace—something I longed for. Some said it came from their living, caring Creator God. So, one night in desperation I cried out, "If there is a living, true God, then please show me—help me!"

Grace saw I was distressed and was in no shape to care for Honey. She called her sister Gik in Phu Sang, Thailand, who was the co-founder of the Village of Hope for abandoned, abused, and at-risk, vulnerable children. Grace sent a picture of me holding Honey. When Gik looked deep into our eyes, she cried and said, "How can we not help, even though we have no means to care for such a young baby!"

Gik and her husband, Pratuan, drove four hours to Chiang Mai to take Honey. When they arrived at the home, they were kind, but when they held Honey, she cried. Gik said, "Oh, the baby does not know me, and she will cry the four hours back home. Please travel with us and stay one week to get Honey settled. Then you can leave if you wish, but please travel with us." I remembered how it felt to be all alone as a small child, so for Honey's sake I reluctantly said yes. Gik sat in the back seat playing and talking with Honey and me. There was no condemnation, just an unusual calmness in their spirits and in their quiet, gentle words. I sensed very quickly that something was different.

We arrived at the Village of Hope around four in the afternoon. It was nothing like I expected. At first glance, I saw a huge, wide-open yard with kids playing on the playground and beautiful new school buildings with kids running free and laughing! When we stepped out of the car, kids came running from everywhere calling out, "Papa Pratuan, Mom Gik, we missed you!" Kids ran up, giving them hugs, and when they saw Honey and me, we were greeted the same way. I simply could not understand—they did not know me or Honey. Why would they greet us with hugs and smiles? They immediately captured Honey's attention and had her laughing. Her eyes just lit up! I wondered, "What is this place?" I thought Mom Gik had said many of the kids were abandoned, high-risk like me. I wondered if they had those kids hiding somewhere else because all these children seemed very happy!

At the Village of Hope there are eight homes on campus. Honey and I were given our own room in the Glen Este Home of Hope set aside especially for teen girls with children and for house moms and teachers in the school. I thought Honey would take a nap after such a long trip, but she could still hear the children playing and laughing. She just wanted to explore. It was that afternoon that I met another teen mom named Sa and her young son, Peter. She welcomed me into her life and her story right away. Sa had a glow about her and a beautiful smile, even after all she had been through. Peter was almost one year older than Honey. He was "all boy" and a handful, but he kept Honey delightfully entertained. I discovered that parts of Sa's story were similar to mine. For the first time in my life, I felt I had someone to talk to who understood me. However, what I did not yet understand was the peace and joy Sa possessed.

Broken Chains, Broken Cycle Healed

That one week I had promised to stay at the Village of Hope for Honey's transition turned into two weeks—then four weeks, then nine months. ... The genuine love of the people and the children kept me there. It was during that ninth month that I realized that God had answered my prayer, "God if you are real, show me—help me!" I received Christ as my living Lord and was baptized. I embraced a heavenly Father Who loved me unconditionally and would never leave me nor forsake me.

I finally had a real family! Even though I was sixteen years old and had a baby, I went back to school and finished. For several years, I was a cook at the Village of Hope and had a steady income. I now have a good job in a nearby city.

I'm happy that Honey is able to have a free, quality Christian education at Lana Christian School. This is something I would have never been able to provide. She is learning she has a heavenly Father who loves her and will never forsake her. Honey just finished first grade and is even learning to speak English. She has a wonderful future ahead of her. She is loved, wanted, and accepted by all the children, teachers, and leaders—again, something I never had.

I discovered family is not always created by blood, but is bound by love.

Hard "rains" can be devastating, but at the Village of Hope, I soon realized that rain can also nurture and bring forth hope for new life.

— *Rain*

Heart Challenge

It is the LORD your God who goes with you. He will not leave you or abandon you. (Deut. 31:6)

We pray you too will discover the God Who sees and hears when you've been mistreated, when you find yourself in the desert feeling all alone, when you can't go on. We pray you have the faith and courage to cry out to the God Who will never leave you without hope.

CHAPTER SEVEN

LITTLE PINK *dress of* FAITH

> For the needy shall not always be forgotten,
> and the hope of the poor shall not perish
> forever. (Psa. 9:18)

POVERTY'S PERFECT STORM

Poverty creates a snowball effect that puts vulnerable children at risk, with many being abandoned, abused, and exploited. When you combine poverty with a lack of education and thousands of years of dark but accepted foolish cultural practices, these create a perfect storm. This destructive path affects children generation to generation.

After completing a four-day Secret Women's Retreat with courageous women of persecution, our small American team of ladies thought we were basically finished with the task God sent us to do. However, we quickly discovered God was secretly unfolding His own main mission to answer the secret prayer of a little six-year-old girl.

Beautiful, harmonizing voices of praise echoed across the swaying rice fields as our team of ladies excitedly packed a bag full of crafts to share with Compassionate Hope's Mercy Care children's ministry.

Compassionate Hope Mercy Care assists abandoned, single moms or widowed grandmothers caring for their children or abandoned grandchildren. These are women who have housing and a meager job but need a little help so they can continue raising their children at home. Saturday Praise Camp was filled with giggles and hugs as the team interacted with crafts, music, dramatized Bible lessons, and provided for a good, hot meal to fill the children's tummies.

> But Jesus called them to him, saying, "Let
> the children come to me, and do not hinder

them, for to such belongs the kingdom of
God." (Luke 18:16)

LITTLE BAYAH

During the praise time, a man walked in carrying his
three-year-old daughter and sat in the very back of the
room. Immediately, two of our Home of Hope girls, sisters
named Mesua and Maling, ran over and started loving on
the little girl. Through translators, we understood that the
visiting man was Mesua and Maling's biological father!
He had brought the girls' baby sister, Bayah, with him.
Six-year-old Mesua and eight-year-old Maling had been
living in Compassionate Hope's Home of Hope in Phu
Sang, Thailand, for seven months. That day the little sister
excitedly joined the group fun with her big sisters.

We discovered the father's purpose for coming was to
see if the Home of Hope would now receive three-year-
old Bayah as well. Our minds and hearts were filled with
questions. What circumstances would drive a father to give
away all three of his daughters? That was a hard concept
for us American moms to understand. My husband, Al, and
our key national leader, Pratuan, father of the home, were
away in the mountains on another mission and were unable
to be contacted for an immediate decision. So, the father
placed little Bayah in front of him on the motorcycle and
drove away. A fun-filled day turned heavy-hearted with
concern for the fate of this little sister.

LITTLE RESCUE

I will not leave you as orphans; I will come to
you. (John 14:18)

The next twenty-four hours were filled with more questions, prayers, and decisions. A rescue plan for Bayah was put in place for Sunday right after church. The Phu Sang Home of Hope's key leaders, Al and I, our American volunteers, and sisters Mesua and Maling all squeezed into two vans in search of little Bayah. We traveled dusty, curvy back roads toward the family home where Mom Gik had first received Mesua and Maling. The girls happily sang songs of praise as we traveled. Silently I (Susan) was thinking that only seven months ago these two little girls were delivered from extreme poverty and horrific, at-risk situations and Buddhist teachings. Now, they are singing songs of praise to a living, loving heavenly Father. It was obvious that the Home of Hope had already made a major difference in their little hearts.

While traveling, we gathered more of the background story as to what would drive a father to give up all three of his daughters. He was from Laos and had migrated over to Thailand to find better work and housing to provide for his wife and seven children. A man concerned for the children gave him permission to put up a temporary little bamboo hut on his property. However, the father discovered that, without a proper visa, he could only find low-paying, manual labor jobs in rice fields and on rubber plantations, making less than four dollars a day. During the rice off-season there was no work. One day he told his wife to stay with the kids while he went back to Laos to secure a job and housing; then he would return for them.

The wife didn't hear from her husband for months. With each passing day she felt more hopeless. Every day, this mom tirelessly searched for ant eggs, grasshoppers, bugs, mushrooms, leaves—anything to make some watery soup to feed her starving children.

Seven months later, her husband returned with a new, pregnant wife and her three teenage boys—and still he had no job! As you can imagine, the first, exhausted wife was distraught—and for good reason! She had sacrificed and nearly starved to death herself, just to keep her family together in hopes of her husband's return. Now, she would have to share her husband and have even less food for her own kids in order to help feed another family of five!

Culturally, there is something else she knew. The second wife and her children were all older and more domineering than she and her children, which meant one thing—the second wife was now in control. Everyone else would be her slaves. Heartbroken, hopeless, and distraught, Bayah's mom slipped out of the hut that night, leaving everyone behind and she never returned.

Maling and Mesua came into the Homes at the Village of Hope because they were "at-risk" of slavery and abuse from their older stepbrothers and stepmom. Soon after, the father saw similar signs and realized that three-year-old Bayah was also in grave danger. It is hard to understand why the men in these cultural situations don't stand up to abuse.

We find a similar story in the Bible. King David didn't stand up and fight the incestuous abuse against his own daughter, Tamar, by her half-brother! Through the Compassionate Hope Homes of Hope, we are fighting hard to train the next generation of young men to break the invisible chains of the "Tamar Syndrome of Silence" that plagues almost every family in Thailand, especially in the poverty-stricken hill tribes. But let's be realistic; it happens here in the Western world as well.

Speak up for those who cannot speak for themselves, for the rights of all who are destitute. Speak up and judge fairly; defend the rights of the poor and needy. (Prov. 31:8–9 NIV)

LITTLE HUT

When we finally reached the tiny bamboo hut where Mesua and Maling once lived, it started pouring down rain. The scene inside is still vividly etched in my mind. As we stepped inside and stood on the dirt floor, rain was seeping in from the sides. I think our entire team was trying to imagine what it would have been like for Mesua and Maling to have lived here with nine other siblings.

As our eyes scanned the dimly lit hut, we saw the kitchen consisted only of one large dirty, black cast iron pot, still sitting in the ashes from an open fire. In the far corner were two makeshift beds made with bamboo sticks tied together with string, with only a quarter-inch straw mat to sleep on. A few clothes hung from the leaking tin ceiling. The girls excitedly led the way to a pile of dirty clothes on the far bed, digging and each finding an old skirt they once wore. They shook off the dust and held the skirts to their waists smiling, as if they each had found a lost treasure.

The only pictures in the hut were of Mesua and Maling at their K-5 graduations. Mesua was jumping up and down to see her picture hanging from a rafter! As one of the volunteers reached for it, a huge spider as big as the palm of her hand crawled out from behind it, and we all screamed! This spider was just a symbol that made us more aware of the unseen, lurking threats in the home.

We heard the rumble of a motorcycle drive up. As the father stepped into the hut, he barely acknowledged his daughters.

He told us that he had temporarily moved his family to the rubber tree plantation where he worked. So, off we went.

BIG LITTLE RESCUE

We arrived at the plantation, but the stepmother had all the kids working in the rice fields. While the dad left to retrieve little Bayah, another unexpected scene unfolded. When Mesua and Maling stepped out of the van, they spotted a woman standing in the doorway. They ran to give hugs and tears were flowing. At first, we thought perhaps their mother had returned, but it was their dad's sister who was there visiting a few days. She sobbed, saying she thought she would never see the girls again. We told her she was always welcome to visit the girls at the Homes of Hope.

The following hour of events was heart-wrenching, and we were all a hot, sobbing, broken, emotional mess! Words can never describe witnessing firsthand the separating of a family, even though you know it may be what is best for the child.

The sound of the motorcycle echoed as it wound its way through the rubber trees, and our hearts were beating with anticipation of what was to come. What a sweet reunion for the three sisters when they saw each other, but to Mesua and Maling's surprise, off the back of the motorcycle came not only Bayah, but their four-year-old little brother, Noah, too.

What a joyous reunion for all four siblings, jumping up and down and holding each other so tightly. All of us were smiling and crying at the same time! Mesua was carrying little Noah around and excitedly introducing us to this little guy whose smile spread from ear to ear.

Our team took turns getting to know the children while Pastor Pratuan, Mom Gik, and Papa Al engaged in important and necessary conversations. The father, holding back glassy tears, was very firm that this was the best decision for Bayah's protection. The aunt emerged, fighting the care-filled tears streaming down her brown cheeks, as she handed me a tiny plastic grocery bag of clothes with two pairs of panties and one pant set. I gave her a hug as we both tried to hide our tears from the girls. It was clear that none of us really wanted the scene unfolding in front of us, but love, poverty, and unbelievable yet accepted cultural traditions that feed man's lust, incest, and abuse were all leading characters driving the climax of this real-life drama!

LEAVING LITTLE NOAH

It was time to head back to the Home of Hope. Surprisingly, there were no tears from any of the three girls as they said goodbye to their father. I was carrying Bayah and her tiny bag of clothes in my arms. As I was about to step into the van, I noticed Noah by my side as well. I whispered to Al behind me, "Al, Noah thinks he is going with us too." We couldn't know what was going through his four-year-old little mind, but that big white van probably looked like an exciting adventure with his sisters. It also showed us how children could be easily enticed into hands for evil and not good. I swallowed hard as I watched Al pick up Noah and hand him to one of our team members to be delivered back to his father. The stepmom had sent Noah in hopes we would take him, too! However, our home for boys was not yet complete, and we also knew that Noah, being a little boy, was not in immediate danger of sexual abuse.

LITTLE HANDS, LITTLE FEET

As we drove away toward the Homes of Hope with Bayah cuddled in my lap, and Mesua and Maling snuggled between Al and me, there are three scenes etched into my mind that I will never forget.

Bayah was hot and sticky, so I gave her a bottle of water, which she quickly drank from and shared with her giggling, happy sisters. I asked around for wet wipes from the team, and soon Al and I were tenderly washing the red, clay dirt from the rice field from Bayah's precious face, little hands, and feet. As Al and I washed Bayah's little feet, we were humbled that God had granted us the privilege of fulfilling that sacred act of love that Jesus spoke of when He washed the disciples' feet in John 13. My eyes locked with Al's as we embraced this shared moment, knowing that this child's life would now forever be changed. The team graciously shared snacks with Bayah and her sisters. The next thing I knew, Bayah was sound asleep in my arms, and my mother's heart wished I could hold her forever.

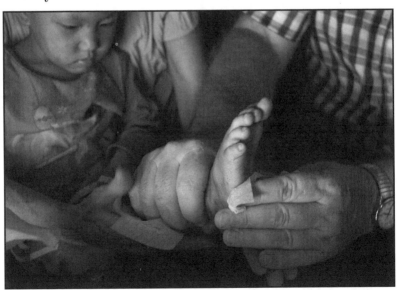

LITTLE TEARS, BIG PROMISE

It had been a very long day, so we stopped for gas, snacks, and a restroom break. Everyone piled out but me. I was not about to awaken the little "sleeping beauty" in my arms. Six-year-old Mesua and Pastor Pratuan were the first back into the van. In the quiet moment, Pastor Pratuan spoke to Mesua in Thai and asked, "Mesua, are you happy to have your little sister with you now?" She gently laid her head on his shoulder and expressed words from her little, tender heart that I will never forget: "My joy is not yet full till I have my baby Noah with me!" I swallowed hard, trying to fight back my own tears, and drew her close till the team returned.

The excitement had calmed, but clearly the emotional reality of the day caught up with Mesua as steady tears began to flow from her eyes, expressing the loss in her heart. The team returned to the van, and when Al saw Mesua's flowing tears, I shared her tender words with him. He drew her beside him, brushing away her tears, and softly asked, "Mesua, do you believe that Papa Al and Pastor Pratuan love you?" Mesua nodded her head saying, "Yes!" He asked Mesua to look into his eyes and said, "Mesua, we told your dad that as soon as we get the monies to finish the Home of Hope for boys, Papa Al and Pastor Pratuan promised that we would all go back and get little Noah! OK? I promise!" Mesua's sobbing stopped. She hugged her Papa Al and smiled from ear to ear. Cheers and awe arose from the team in release from this pivotal, emotional moment, awakening our newest, little princess! Wiping her tears and smiling, Mesua pulled Bayah from my lap and into her arms, holding her tightly.

Trauma is real for these little rescued ones, but true love and a safe home give new meaning to hope and unconditional love.

Can a woman forget her nursing child, that she should have no compassion on the son of her womb? Even these may forget, yet I will not forget you. Behold, I have engraved you on the palms of my hands. (Isa. 49:15–16a)

LITTLE PINK DRESS OF FAITH

All that Al and I have accomplished in life, we clearly realize was simply God using us as instruments in response to someone else's silent prayers. What happened next confirms that very thought and revealed a hidden, but big prayer of big faith from a little heart that resulted in a BIG answer!

It was late afternoon when we arrived back at the Village of Hope. The house moms and all the girls excitedly came out to welcome their newest little sister. Mesua and Maling were proudly introducing Bayah to everyone, and her little brown eyes were just dancing, taking it all in. After an emotional, rollercoaster day, it was such a relief to witness this beautiful, welcoming transition.

Mesua grabbed Bayah's little hand as they entered the home and excitedly said, "Come, come, Bayah! Come see what I have for you!" Mesua led her baby sister to a little chest, and boldly proclaimed, "Bayah, I have been praying and praying that God would someday bring you here to live with us in the Home of Hope so you could be safe." From the bottom drawer, Mesua pulled out the cutest little pink dress just Bayah's size! Out of the mouth of this precious six-year-old came the most profound words of faith I've ever heard from a child:

"Look," said Mesua, "I have been saving clothes for you—so when God brought you here you would have new, clean clothes!" Did you get that? So WHEN God brought you here! Wow, now that is faith in action!

Bayah started jumping up and down with joy, and the other two sisters joined! Maling, the oldest, grabbed both sisters' hands and said, "Come, let's get cleaned up!"

Oh, how all our hearts melted as we overheard the nonstop giggles and laughter that echoed from the shower room as they splished and splashed. Later, out walked three squeaky-clean, smiling faces, and Bayah in her cute "little pink dress of faith."

LITTLE FAITH LESSON

Mesua's mustard seed faith did not wait for God to move "the mountain" of separation. She actively prepared by saving the little pink dress by faith for WHEN God did move the mountain! What a lesson we learned that day from a six-year-old that convicted and stirred our own hearts. She did not simply pray about it; she acted on it in faith. How does God want you to actively prepare for answered prayer?

> For I was hungry and you gave me food, I was thirsty and you gave me drink, I was a stranger and you welcomed me, I was naked and you clothed me.... Then the righteous will answer Him, saying, "Lord, when did we see you ...?" And the King [Jesus] will answer them, "Truly, I say to you, as you did it to one of the least of these my brothers [or sisters], you did it to me." (Matt. 25:35–36b, 37, 40)

LITTLE NOAH'S WELCOME

Three months later, the first boys' Home of Hope was finally finished. Papa Al returned and a promise was kept. Mesua's prayer and joy were complete when her baby brother Noah was lovingly welcomed into the family at the Compassionate Hope's Homes of Hope very first boys' home in Phu Sang. This was only possible because of incredible and dedicated national leaders working together with faithful home sponsors! It was a time of celebration and joy unspeakable: a promise kept, a prayer answered, and JOY that was finally FULL!

> And whoever gives one of these little ones even a cup of cold water because he is a disciple, truly, I say to you, he will by no means lose his reward. (Matt. 10:42)

Heart Challenge

RISK A LITTLE LOVE

Without caring people, these vulnerable children would have fallen into the hands of evil humanity and more abuse. What a joy to be partners together in God's plan to rescue and restore hope by helping to rewrite a future for each child. Passionately seated deep within our hearts by the Holy Spirit is the knowledge that each one of these children is a priceless treasure. They are the created sons and daughters of God. They deserve to be valued and given the best opportunity possible to fulfill God's eternal purpose for their lives.

People often say, "Oh, I could never go because I would want to bring all the children back home with me." We say, "Oh, you are right! But that will only be your first response. I will tell you what it will really do...."

It will make your heart beat with deeper compassion. Your arms will stretch wider to give and embrace more love. Your feet will run faster to follow harder after Christ for the sake of others. Your faith will be challenged and grow stronger, and your prayers bolder! But, most of all, it will loosen your grip on the insignificant things of life that you thought were most important so that the "least of these" know they are significant and worth your love.

So go, risk love, and let love change you so you can be a part of changing their future!

LEARN MORE ABOUT BAYAH'S RESCUE

www.CompassionateHope.org/bayahs-story

CHAPTER EIGHT

REDEEMED *to set* OTHERS FREE

For their Redeemer is mighty; he shall plead their cause with thee. (Prov. 23:11 KJV)

POWER OF REDEMPTION

The story of redemption is always set on the backdrop of loss, pain, and ruin. However, when Jesus, our Kinsman-Redeemer, steps in to rescue, He turns ashes into beauty, mourning into joy, and heaviness into praise (Isa. 61:3).

Each time we sit in the assessment process with a newly rescued child in the Homes of Hope and hear their life story, it breaks our hearts. It can be a roller coaster ride of emotions and questions, even in our own minds, as we try to discern the next step for them. Each child that we receive into our hearts as our own has experienced some type of tragic loss or deep wounds. As leaders, sometimes in our weak flesh, our first reaction can be, "God, how are You ever going to heal and redeem such pain?" Our

second reaction is to cry out, "Mercy, mercy, Lord, mercy for this child!" Witnessing the track record of the power of redemption is what keeps us and our Compassionate Hope leaders listening and loving unconditionally again and again.

An old friend of ours, Roy Hession, gave the best explanation of redemption, which has been a "North Star" for us. Below is a summary thought from his wonderful little book, *Our Nearest Kinsman* (pages 3–4). This book is filled with golden nuggets to mine.

> REDEEM: to buy back with a price—(Jesus, our true Redeemer) overrules that which was lost or forsaken, or caused or occasioned by our sin, or by the sin of others.

Redemption always costs somebody something!

NING'S FREEDOM AND REDEMPTION STORY

The theme of the power of redemption is woven into the very fabric of Ning's story. It is a story of a God Who seeks what was lost, redeems that which was forsaken, and gives grace to forgive the unforgivable. It is a story that causes you to be lost in the wonder of Who God is and what He has done. It is a cry that vibrates from the depth of every hurting soul filled with loss. It is a song that echoes in every heart: "Let the hopeless find hope; let the rejected find love; let the broken be healed, and let those bound in invisible chains be set free!" (Susan).

> He heals the brokenhearted and binds up their wounds. (Psa. 147:3)

With one hand, Al and I pen Ning's story. With the other, we reach for yours and pray that together we will discover the power of redemption in our own lives.

JUST NING

I am Ning. I am thirty-one years old. I was born in Bangkok, Thailand, but raised in a small village in Laos. Our family was very poor. Showers consisted of simply a bucket of water poured over our heads. As a little girl, I grew up full of fear. My father was an alcoholic, which brought constant conflict and abuse, especially toward my mother. When troubles started, I would grab my little sister and hide because we knew we would be next. I still have traumatizing memories of watching my drunken father waving a knife in his hand as he screamed death threats!

When I was eleven, I became a very beautiful young girl. Men began to want me. My fifth-grade teacher would find excuses to keep me after school. He intentionally failed me so he could be with me one more year, and he threatened me not to tell anyone. I was frozen, chained in fear, and clothed in shame.

Shame has a voice, and it speaks in small sounds of scornful whispers. It whispers, "Don't speak. Don't tell!" It whispers down at you, "You are of no worth, no value. You did something to deserve this!" I believed its lies!

If you wanted to attend middle or high school in my rural village, you had to travel into the city each day or find a place to board for that year. Like many others, my family did not have the transportation or money for me to continue my education. At this age, many girls from rural areas start to become targets for labor/sex trafficking or sold as child brides. No one talks about it or does anything to prevent it. This is just a culturally hidden but secretly accepted practice: stealing and enslaving innocent lives. I had never heard of labor trafficking, but it soon became my story.

Labor Trafficked

When I was twelve years old, my mom and dad took me out of school, and we moved to Bangkok. My parents and I went to work in a candy factory. My papers were falsified to make it appear that I was older. I was just Ning, a poor girl who was born only to do what others commanded me to do. My parents told me over and over that I had to do this to help our family survive. But honestly, it was no way to "just survive," and it was only the beginning of my hidden desperation.

Working long hours six days a week and making only a few dollars a day, I was extremely tired. The next few years were very fearful and confusing. Unfortunately, I grew up way too fast. I was threatened and sexually abused by the boss's son. There seemed to be a target on my back, and I felt that death would come if I ever told anyone about the abuse. The boss and his son often threatened to fire my parents and put us in prison if I told. The invisible chains were tightening and there were days that I could barely breathe. Hope was choked out of me. I just wanted to be a kid again—to get back in school and finish my education.

One day, I quietly mentioned to my mom a few things that had happened. The next day she went to my boss to stand up for me. Immediately, we found ourselves in jail at the police station. The threats from the boss were now a reality! We were forced to pay an enormous fine because my father had falsified my age on the paperwork. This cost all our savings from our combined salaries. With no money, our family was even extradited back to my father's home country of Laos. Yet, nothing was done about the boss's son abusing me! My mind and soul were tutored that speaking up just caused more pain! I was voiceless.

Signed Away as a Bride

As I matured, my family saw my beauty was an asset, a potential provision for them. I was coerced, this time by my very own family. They told me that it was my duty to provide, or we would not survive. I was told, after all, it was my fault we lost all our money. This cultural-duty mindset is an instilled obligation from birth and an invisible chain that has been passed down for generations.

When I was seventeen years old, a family member—with my parents' permission—sent me to America to marry a much older man whom I did not know or love. I did not want to do this! I hated being constantly brainwashed and seasoned to emotionally and mentally believe that this was my duty and responsibility.

Feeling voiceless and powerless, I eventually caved into their manipulation and signed the contract. After all, I'm just Ning, born to do what I am commanded to do, but deep down it was not what I wanted!

The next three years were beyond difficult, painful, and lonely! Words cannot express the hopelessness I felt, and some days I wished not to live. It was horrible! More than the enslavement of my circumstances, I was dying from the ever-tightening invisible chains on the inside. When I didn't do what the man who purchased me told me to do, he would shake the contract in my face and say, "You have to! You signed the marriage contract!" This was not a marriage because, in reality, I was like contracted property sold on an auction block, still shackled in chains. If my parents really loved me, how could they have allowed this and think it was best for me? They were home, surviving from the money they received while I was dying inside! I felt so alone.

Eventually, when the man thought I could be trusted, he arranged for me to work in a restaurant owned by another family member. I felt that every move I made was monitored. Even though the long hours were hard, it was better than being imprisoned at home.

The owner of the restaurant felt that I needed to learn more English to be a better server. Two days a week, I was allowed to take ESL (English as a Second Language) classes after work. It was only a few blocks from work, so I was allowed to walk to class. This was the only time that I ever felt free. I'm sure you are wondering, "Why did she not run away?" Deep-rooted fear tutored my mind to believe his intimidating threats that he had eyes everywhere, and life had taught me not to trust anyone. From childhood I was seasoned to believe that my true purpose was to serve and care for my family, and I was constantly told that it would be stupid, foolish, and selfish if I ever ran. I was in a foreign country, and in my brainwashed head the list of why I didn't run was endless.

Discerning the Signs

My English was not good, but I studied very hard in my ESL class. We all laughed at our English mistakes. I enjoyed the interaction, being with people, especially one particular teacher who seemed to take a special interest in me. There was something different about her; later I learned that she was a Christian. She kept asking me questions about my life to stir conversational English (I thought), but mostly I kept my secret inside.

This teacher began sharing about her Jesus Who heals broken hearts, and I was curious to know more. The gods in my country were carved statues overlaid with gold, which never made much sense to me. How could a statue of wood ever help me? Eventually, I felt safe with my teacher and began sharing tiny pieces of my story with her, until one day I poured out my trouble.

Feeling all along that something was not right, my teacher wasn't shocked. She knew that we needed wisdom and discernment to know how to move forward. I felt that she really cared about me and didn't want something in return. Now, I am so thankful for someone who was discerning and realized the symptoms and signs and took a risk in loving me!

My ESL teacher and a discerning Asian man who frequented the restaurant kept encouraging me to be brave and secretly told me they would help when I was ready. Eventually, I was assisted to track down a pastor in Thailand that I was told could help. I eventually got up the courage to secretly give him a call. It was a long shot, but I told him and his wife my story.

> I will deliver you out of the hand of the wicked, and redeem you from the grasp of the ruthless. (Jer. 15:21)

Strategic Rescue Plans

This caring Thai pastor called his mentor and spiritual father, "Papa Al," who helps to rescue children in Thailand. Papa Al embraced my story, and through several means God provided the funding. Then we all began to put a detailed, strategic, secret rescue plan in place. I was so terrified that someone at the restaurant or home would find out the plan before I could escape. What I didn't know was that many people from all over the world were praying for my protection and escape. I just kept my regular routine and tried to do everything as I was told.

The Escape Route

I hid my passport in my purse along with my secret tip money; I didn't even pack a bag. I went to work as normal, trying not to show on the outside how nervous I was, but I was definitely shaking on the inside. My thoughts were: "What if I get caught?" Imagining what evil would happen to me, I concluded it could not be much worse than living in the invisible death row prison I was already in. I took the risk!

Leaving work, I started walking toward my normal route for my ESL class. Around the corner I saw a taxi waiting as arranged. Doubts flooded my mind, as I wondered if this was another trap. I stood there shaking! Taking a deep breath as if about to dive into deep water, I ran to the taxi and off to the airport we sped! I had never gone through check-in at an airport by myself and didn't know if my English would be enough to understand. I secured a phone before leaving and was able to secretly text my moves. Although I was not aware, people were praying me through each step, each check-point, and each airport. After making it through Tokyo, I felt I could breathe a little bit; however, fear was still present. On the flight descending to Bangkok, I began wondering if any family member was contacted about my disappearance and might be waiting at the Bangkok airport to take me away.

Thirty-one hours after getting into the taxi in America, I met the Thai pastor and his wife with smiles in Bangkok. Overwhelmed, I fell weeping into their arms! They had driven over twelve hours to meet me. The next day, this precious couple took me into their home and hearts, welcoming me as their own daughter. I'm so grateful for all those who were a part of my secret rescue story! If they had not helped, I would not be here to tell my story.

> Rescue me, O my God, from the hand of the wicked, from the grasp of the unjust and cruel man. For you, O Lord, are my hope. (Psa. 71:4–5a)

Rescued Soul

Together, everyone helped me to come to know Jesus—
my true Rescuer, Redeemer, and Healer of my soul and
fears.

*I remember feeling loved by God, and
knew that He saw me and heard my
desperate cries for help.*

For the first time, I was experiencing God's love, which was
fresh and new! I wanted more, so I fasted for twenty days
to draw near to Him. In God's presence I sensed His forgiveness and cleansing, giving me a new life, inside and out.
I had real hope for the first time in my life!

> Is not this the kind of fasting I have chosen:
> to loose the chains of injustice and untie the
> cords of the yoke, to set the oppressed free
> and break every yoke?... Then your light will
> break forth like the dawn, and your healing
> will quickly appear; then your righteousness
> will go before you, and the glory of the Lord
> will be your rear guard. (Isa. 58:6, 8 NIV)

Instead of becoming bitter, I deeply felt so thankful for all
that had brought me to Jesus!

> I love the LORD, because he has heard my
> voice and my pleas for mercy. Because he
> inclined his ear to me, therefore I will call on
> him as long as I live. (Psa. 116:1-2)

When I first returned to Thailand, my parents and aunt
were all very angry at me. They said, "How could you be so

stupid that you would give up this money and security for us and our family?" They did not speak to me or try to help me for several years.

Words can never express how deeply this hurt me, so I just clung to Jesus and hoped that He would heal my heart. I realized that even though I was abandoned by my family, I was embraced by Jesus and my new family of God. I found great joy in serving people, especially children and young girls who were like me.

> For you have been my help, and in the shadow of your wings I will sing for joy. My soul clings to you; your right hand upholds me. (Psa. 63:7-8)

Forgiveness

About six months later, I heard Papa Al speak for the first time in a discipleship gathering for Christian leaders. I was drawn to his wisdom and love of Jesus, and I asked many questions. That night, I suddenly realized that he was one of many who helped in my escape! Because I could speak some broken English, I was able to tell him thank you. He listened to me and truly cared about who I was. He saw me, and through him, a deeper healing and restoration began.

Papa Al also helped me begin to deal with unforgiveness. I eventually was able to reach back and extend love and forgiveness to my own parents and family, and they saw that I was different. As I extended unconditional love and grace, my mom's and sister's hearts softened. I told them of the One Who changed my life, and they too received Jesus as their Lord and Redeemer. Everywhere possible, I told others how they too could be set free!

> Be kind to one another, tenderhearted, forgiving one another, as God in Christ forgave you. (Eph. 4:32)

Rescue Others

Ten months later, Papa Al was back in my city for another discipleship training conference. One day as my adopted family and I sat at lunch with Papa Al, he asked me to share some of my story. I will never forget the question he asked, "Ning, what do you want to do with your life?" I wept! No one ever cared enough to see me as valuable enough to have a God-given purpose. Papa Al encouraged me to begin to consider the Lord's purpose for my life, based upon all that I had experienced. Through him, Mom Susan, and others on the Compassionate Hope team, I began to believe that I had significance, worth, and value. By faith, I believed that God had a special plan for my life.

With the help of Compassionate Hope, I was able to touch my passion to help young teen girls who were at risk and trapped like I had been. I wanted girls to never go through what I did, but rather have a good education that I never had, so they would be able to have hope and dream of a future. The accepted cultural cycle of abuse with its chains of hopelessness is an epidemic in our region and must be broken! I began to believe that with God's grace— along with the help and training from others—I could make a difference in other girls' lives. At first, even some Christian men said that I was weak, uneducated, and just a young, poor female, and they said I could not do this. However, Papa Al and Mom Susan have become like a second dad and mom to me. They became my mentors and believed in me, and said, "Ning, yes, you can! You will make mistakes; we all do, but you will learn. You have God's heart, and God's hand is upon you!"

> Rescue the weak and the needy; deliver them from the hand of the wicked. (Psa. 82:4)

Homes of Hope

Through the years, Compassionate Hope has been committed to train and help me fulfill my dream to rescue girls. We celebrate because we have now opened the first Home of Hope in my province. This city is a strategic location for a Home because it is a border crossing town, and many children and women are trafficked through it every day.

Our prayer and dream to purchase land just came true, for which we give praise to God! As funds come in, we pray to build more Homes of Hope to give new life to more children. As we do build, we will also need more workers, sponsors, and volunteers. However, for these first ten girls, they now have a safe home of love, preventing them from going through many of the hurts and pains I experienced. I helped them to find the love of Jesus at a younger age than I did. I am teaching them English, and some Saturdays we all go into rural villages to teach English classes, which open doors to tell others about Jesus. These girls love to sing of their Rescuer, Jesus, because they know He is their true Father, Who will never leave, forsake, or abuse them. I have taught them to speak openly and freely from their hearts before Him, and that He will hear their cry. From this Home, some have gone on to college or technical training and careers.

Chains Broken

I love watching the girls grow in Christ's love and discover their true identity in Christ because their pasts dictated a different picture. These are my beautiful, happy, chosen daughters! Each is special, and I love them as my very own. Several years ago, I received the "Mother of the Year" award at their public school. People in the community are watching and seeing how love truly makes a difference. Today, this uneducated, poor girl travels through different countries as a translator, telling others my God story of a Redeemer Who can overrule our losses and turn them into good. My chains are broken and are being used as an invisible key to unlock the chains of others, so they too can be set free like my oldest daughter of my heart, Kon.

Kon's Rescue

One day, I received word of a teen girl being labor and sex trafficked by her stepfather at a hotel construction site very near our Home of Hope. Every day in ninety-degree heat, this young girl carried gravel and concrete, all the while experiencing lustful stares and shameful remarks from the men. At age sixteen, Kon was rescued and brought into our Home of Hope and into my heart. Slowly, she felt safe and healing began. Sharing parts of my own story gave her the courage to unlock a secret that tied our pasts together.

> Let the redeemed of the LORD tell their story—those he redeemed from the hand of the foe. (Psa. 107:2 NIV)

On Kon's seventeenth birthday, she received her very first birthday cake ever! As a family, we celebrated who she was! That day was filled with tears of joy, but at the end of the night she opened up to me, revealing a "silent secret fear." A dark, hidden door cracked open as tearfully she shared that her family had already contracted her to be the wife of the construction owner, for whom she had worked. Her stepfather had already received the money and, on her eighteenth birthday, she would be turned over to that horrible old man to become his third wife. Kon wailed while I held her in my arms as we cried together! Through prayers and much coaching over the weeks ahead, Papa Al and I "couraged up" Kon. We explained that we would protect her and that the contract was illegal, even though it was accepted by culture. We further assured her that, because she was now under the care of Compassionate Hope, her stepfather and the construction man would be put in jail if they attempted to take her by force.

Without knowing it, sharing my own past experience of being coerced and given away as a bride to an older man by my parents released Kon from an invisible chain and set her free. Just before her eighteenth birthday, she had the strength to confront her parents and the man, and boldly proclaimed, "No!" Kon was finally free.

This past New Year's Eve, Kon's mom came to the Home of Hope. During the worship celebration, we each shared thankfulness for our blessings. The Gospel was woven through each testimony from the youngest to the oldest of the girls. That night Kon's mother fell into her daughter's arms as she too received the Lord and asked Kon's forgiveness! New hope and life were birthed—pain, sorrow, loss, and sin redeemed! Kon and her mom recently moved into a small house together not far from us! Now twenty-one years old, Kon is finishing up Vo-Tech college.

Big Dreams

Through this Home of Hope, my daughters have a wonderful and different future! They are dreaming big because each one, like Kon, is promised an education beyond high school. This is something they would never have, without the faithful caring supporters of Compassionate Hope.

> All these blessings will come on you and accompany you if you obey the LORD your God. (Deut. 28:2 NIV)

Freed to Free Others

Each day in our Home of Hope, I marvel at the power of God's unfailing love, goodness, and redemption. God has overruled so many losses, so much pain in all of our lives, but He is turning it to good. My story is similar to Joseph's, who was sold into slavery by his own family. However, when he had the chance to return evil, he responded with a heart of forgiveness and set them free.

> You meant it for evil, but God meant it for
> good to accomplish what is now being done,
> the saving of many lives. (Gen. 50:20 NIV)

God is using me now to save many lives! I am truly lost in the wonder of my God!

Please pray for us. In the last few months, we have rescued two sisters. Please encourage us; please love them. Please love me.

I now know that I am NOT "just Ning." I am a daughter of the Most High King! I am set free to free others!

With a grateful heart,

— *Ning*

God is our true Rescuer and Redeemer! To paraphrase Roy Hession again, God sometimes gives back far more than what was lost or forsaken, so that we can be lost in the wonder of Who He is and what He has done.

Heart Challenge

Every day women, children, and young men across the world are being traumatized, abused, and sold. It is a global epidemic. Our heart breaks with yours if you have personally felt its impact. We want you to know you are not alone in your own healing journey!

My dear friend, come to Jesus, the Healer of your soul. Like Ning, learn to speak to God from an open heart and bring your pain all to Him. He is the only One Who can truly heal the sting of shame and sin brought upon your soul. Perhaps you may still be chained to fear and feel the bondage of insignificance like Ning. All of that is a lie! You are precious in God's sight. How do I know? I invite you to look to the cross where Jesus, our suffering Savior, Himself entered into your pain. The cross is a reminder that He loved YOU enough to die for YOU, to cover all your sin, shame, and pain. Don't look back at the past or listen to the words and actions of others. Look to the true love of Christ. Jesus rose from the dead to bring new life! YOU are that valuable!

I pray that someday, like Ning, you too can truly embrace the ability to forgive without expecting anything in return. Forgiveness sets you free! You don't have to live life chained to the past. Jesus is the Chain Breaker! Trust Him. He loved you enough to die for you, to set you free.

If God is speaking to you right now, just lift your voice and cry out loud to Him and say, "Lord, by faith I choose you, and I choose to be set free!" I hear chains falling, don't you?

Receive healing, and in turn, give it away. Yes, give it away! God wants us to realize that healing and comfort from Him is a GIFT that is to be paid forward.

There are two tiny connecting words in 2 Corinthians 1:3–4 that tell us why:

> The Father of mercies and God of all comfort, who comforts us in all our affliction, SO THAT we may be able to comfort those who are in any affliction with the comfort with which we ourselves are comforted by God. (emphasis added)

God desires all of us to be comforting, restoring, healers! Help us to help Ning and other house moms. By doing so, the abandoned, abused, and trafficked children can find healing as well. Your choice to make a difference will enable them to dream big and have a hopeful future!

We at Compassionate Hope have set our focus on being chain breakers and to raise up a new generation of leaders. Join us in being a chain breaker.

In America for suspicious activity, CALL the National Human Trafficking HOTLINE: 1-888-373-7888, or call 911.

FOR MORE ABOUT NING AND THE GIRLS SHE IS CARING FOR AT HER HOME OF HOPE, VISIT:

www.CompassionateHope.org/nings-story

CHAPTER NINE

HIDDEN
in plain
SIGHT

PART 1

FIGHTING INJUSTICE WITH HOPE

Have you ever been robbed, mistreated, violated, or felt powerless? Have you witnessed an injustice and weren't sure what to do? What does the Lord say about it?

> Thus says the Lord, "Do justice and righteousness, and deliver from the hand of the oppressor him who has been robbed. And do no wrong or violence to the resident alien, the fatherless, and the widow, nor shed innocent blood in this place. (Jer. 22:3)

Have you ever been astonished at an injustice and knew you had to intervene, speak up, or do something?

> The Lord looked and was displeased to find there was no justice. He was amazed [astonished] to see that no one intervened to help the oppressed. So he himself stepped in to save them with his strong arm and HIS justice sustained him. (Isa. 59:15b–16 NLT, emphasis added)

If you read on further, you see that God suited up and readied Himself for the battle. Why?

Because God is holy, righteous, and His very character demands that justice rise up! However, His love and compassion also demand mercy and grace. It was at the cross that justice and mercy kissed, and love was offered to the world (Psa. 85:10). He calls us to be His image-bearer, and as His character is engrafted into us so we too are not to sit idly by in comfort and complacency but to stand up for justice, intervene, and step in to show compassion.

WE DON'T "GOT IT"

Have you ever tried to carry on an earnest conversation regarding something heavy on your heart with someone you cared about? Perhaps, like me, it was with a teen heading off to college. Before I finished sharing my heart, they walked away and said, "I got it!" I shook my head inwardly because I knew they really didn't "get it!" So I said, "Wait! Please listen; this is really serious!" I went in for another try, but I was again met with, "I got it, Mom. I got it!" Everything within me wanted to gently turn them around and say, "Look into my eyes. I know you think you 'got it' but please hear me out. This is really serious. Just give me a few more minutes!" Ever been there? I'm smiling at some of you nodding your head!

Today, Al and I are the ones giving the gentle tap on the shoulder to you and the world to say, "Please give us a few more minutes. Please keep reading! This chapter, though hard, is so important!"

Today, we are like the widow in Luke 18 relentlessly knocking on the door of the unjust judge and crying out—"Lord, please—grant justice!" Why?

Our hearts are heavily burdened about a silent epidemic that only a few are talking about—that's why! It is life-threatening and especially ravaging the lives of thousands of Filipino children in its strangling dark web every day. This epidemic is called OSEC or *Online Sexually Exploited Children*. Child pornography is not new, but today in our high-tech world, the demand and supply of abusive live sex shows of children are available with one click. OSEC has quickly become the modern-day face of human trafficking!

You might be thinking: "Well, how does this affect me here in the U.S.?" Yes, the Philippines is at the global epicenter and is the number one country for this horrible injustice. However, the U.S. is the number one country demanding this abuse! When the world went dark during the pandemic lockdown, the dark web for abusive, live sex shows of children lit up the sky and continues to escalate out of control. The pandemic was pivotal in sweeping this hidden epidemic into a catastrophic tsunami.

Startling facts are emerging from the Department of Justice (DOJ) and from watchdogs and data research companies who track these dark web sites. Evidence shows that innocent children are drowning in its deadly undertow every day. It is destroying thousands of Filipino children hidden in plain sight, and this abuse is in a fast downward cultural, generational, moral tailspin. Its curse affects multiple generations and more to come.

> Yet the LORD longs to be gracious to you; therefore he will rise up to show you compassion. For the LORD is a God of justice. Blessed are all who wait for him! (Isa. 30:18 NIV)

We are so thankful for incredible "battle-ready partners" who have stepped up and stepped into this battle with us: the Tim Tebow Foundation, International Justice Mission (IJM), business partners, and various organizations who are on the frontlines with us to fight this injustice with all our might! Will you join us?

> He has shown you, O mortal, what is good. And what does the LORD require of you?

> To act justly and to love mercy and to walk
> humbly with your God. (Mic. 6:8 NIV)

Before we tell you Elly's amazing rescue and redemption story, please give us a few more minutes to explain more of the "why and what." I promise it will help Elly's story be more real and incredible!

WHY THE PHILIPPINES?

There are multiple intertwining reasons that weave this strangling web of death that is OSEC.

The Philippines is a third world country with widespread poverty. You can see children begging on the streets everywhere. Children are taught English in school; thus, high English-speaking proficiency allows other foreign English-speaking countries to manipulate and coerce children into doing whatever evil they request through web cams and cell phones. The lack of education and parents' low-paying jobs make OSEC quick, easy money and children easy prey. The long-standing cultural norms that prioritize supporting family over one's well-being are a strangling noose around the necks of children.

Another reason this is so urgent upon our hearts is that, sadly, seventy percent of these innocent Online Sexually Exploited Children are being abused by family members! Many are abused by their own mothers! This means some of these children are trapped and sentenced to a locked jail cell in their own home with their perpetual abusers. There is nowhere to hide! Their voice is silenced as they cry for help!

Family who should be protecting them use emotional blackmail to make children think it is up to them to make money through these live shows for the family's survival. When mothers are caught, many justify their actions by saying the child had no physical contact with the pedophiles on the screen. However, we know what the foreign viewers see is sometimes not enough, and many travel to the Philippines to act out their abuse in person. But even worse, in these live shows many children are forced to do unthinkable things with other family members, young and old, inside the home.

The country's weak tech infrastructure also creates a roadblock when tracking down the exact location of the perpetrator's IP addresses. Why? Because in the Philippines, twenty-plus people can have the same IP address, and their locations are scattered all over the region. The lack of resources and manpower to track down, rescue, and prosecute the thousands of leads coming in every day slows rescues down.

Age twelve was the consensual age for having sex. The consensual age was moved up to age sixteen in 2020. Sadly, these are only a few excuses. However, no matter the age, cases are very hard to prosecute when traumatized little children are frozen and voiceless to speak against their own mothers and family members.

> Cursed be anyone who perverts the justice due to the sojourner, the fatherless, and the widow. And all the people shall say, "Amen." (Deut. 27:19)

Will you say "Amen" with us?

WHAT FUELS OSEC?

OSEC is fueled by demand and a cheap supply with little consequence. These combined with selfish greed, sexual immorality, and porn addiction are the unquenchable sparks that light the fire. It is said that eight out of ten men struggle with porn addiction and three out of ten women. Today, it is almost an expected norm among teens and young adults, and many start this addiction at around nine to ten years old. Even many pastoral leaders standing in the pulpit struggle. It's time we, the Church, stop complaining about what is outside our doors and stand up, speak out, equip, and deal with the reality within.

For ten years, I (Susan) led a Pure in Heart Conference to help equip moms to plant the seeds of purity in their tween girls' hearts before they reached middle school. I quickly discovered the number one reason parents didn't talk to their children about these issues was their own past failures. We all must push past our own failures to equip our children for the battles ahead and teach them how to protect themselves, especially online. We all fail, but we must model to our children how to "fail forward."

My friend, if the enemy or anyone else tries to bring up your "repentant" past, be assured by this verse:

> But thou hast in love to my soul delivered it
> from the pit of corruption: for thou has cast all
> my sins behind thy back. (Isa. 38:17b KJV)

If a repentant person's sin is behind God's back, who are we to drag it out? This applies to forgiving others, but it also applies to forgiving yourself. Literally, God has it, so let's leave it there.

However, when it comes to the abusive act of child porn and live shows, we all should cringe at this horrible injustice to children. We should ALL stand up and shout "Enough is enough—no more on our watch! This is NOT just an injustice, IT IS A CRIME! A crime against our own humanity—our own children!"

We have often seen that when darkness prevails, children are the first to feel the greater effects.

We at Compassionate Hope grieve over these facts and so should you. We choose to remain in the fight for those still crying in the dark so that we can rescue them, give hope for healing, and make a difference. We choose to stand up and step in to fight for those healing from this horrific trauma.

So, no, we don't fully "get it." I wouldn't "get it" or understand the real urgency if it were not for our caring son Stephen and his Filipino wife, Kathleen, Directors of Compassionate Hope, Philippines, and for all the incredible workers serving there. They tirelessly fight for the lives of rescued OSEC children day and night through our Homes of Hope.

Our Compassionate Hope Foundation Homes are presently the only licensed family-home long-term aftercare facility in all the Philippines to receive OSEC sibling groups.

If one child in a family is being abused, the others are at risk. Our Compassionate Hope grace-filled, trained house parents and social workers are heroes in our eyes. Together, we help some of the neediest, traumatized children on this planet.

Sometimes we wonder how God will break the invisible chains and redeem such emotional soul trauma. There is only one answer, one hope to all this pain: "BUT GOD."

We have witnessed over time the power of His redeeming, healing grace when love and hope step in. One example of this grace is demonstrated in the life of one of our precious rescued girls called Elly.

Elly's story allows you to peek into a tiny window of what it is like for thousands of very broken children trapped in the strangling dark web of OSEC. You will feel the ripple effect as it seeps deep into their wounded souls. However, you will also witness an incredibly courageous girl emerge who discovers her true identity and her voice. She bravely speaks up for those whose voice has been silenced, those still hidden in plain sight. You will also hear her crying out that victory, healing, true love, and hope are possible when people choose to do more than just read her story but bravely run hard into the darkness with the light of Christ to help rescue, redeem, and restore the broken.

> This is what the LORD Almighty said: "Administer true justice; show mercy and compassion to one another." (Zech. 7:9 NIV)

Please note that 50 percent of Elly's story comes from Elly's own healing journal (used with permission but edited into story format) and the rest was scripted from interviews with our caring son Stephen and his beautiful wife Kathleen—Directors of Compassionate Hope, Philippines.

PART 2

HIDDEN IN PLAIN SIGHT: TWO-FACED ELLY

This is Elly's freedom story of hope.

My mom called me "Elly." I was fifteen years old when I was rescued, along with my two sisters and three cousins. The youngest was just a baby. We are all now safe and happy living with our new family at the Village of Hope in the Philippines. But "before," it would be hard for you to believe a life like mine (ours) could even exist.

At nine years old, my mom sent me to live at my aunt's house. At two o'clock one morning, my aunt shook me awake. She said, "Elly, I have a friend, and he wants to say 'hi' to you. He wants you to do a show for him." I was half-asleep and I didn't understand what was happening, but I just tried to obey. Afterwards, I was shaking and sick to my stomach, and was told to go back to bed. I couldn't sleep. I buried my head in the pillow and cried and cried. I just wanted to go back home!

The next morning I was so tired, but I put on a fake smile and tried to act normal at school. That night changed me, and inside I became … "Two-Faced Elly."

This abusive cycle continued for months. I was physically exhausted and so tired of pretending until my mom came and took me home. I was thankful to at last be free from my monster!

The first night, I watched movies and read till I fell asleep.

A few nights later, someone shook me. It scared me, but when the light was turned on, I realized it was my mom. Mom said, "Elly, Elly—wake up! Can you do me a favor?" I felt OK because I knew it was NOT going to be like the "favors" my auntie made me and my cousins do.

Wiping my sleepy eyes, I said, "What is it, Mom?" She said, "Can you say 'hi' to my friend, Peter?" I pulled my blanket tightly toward me as I slowly sat up in bed. "Uh ... who is Peter?" I asked with a sudden knot in my throat. Mom brushed my hair back from my eyes as she handed me the cell phone and very sternly said, "Just say 'hi' and do whatever he says!"

When I saw this foreign man's face smiling at me, my whole world started to crash in around me. I was fighting back the tears and I thought: "This is a dream! Will someone just wake me from this horrible nightmare and rescue me!"

After the "show," my mom left the room, and I broke down sobbing as I fell into bed. I cried out, "How can my own Mom do this horrible thing to me?" I kept thinking, "What am I going to do now? I have no other place to go! I don't even have anyone to tell that I am not safe!"

"Two-Faced Elly" became my life once again, and this time my own mother became my monster at night! My own family was out to destroy me! They stole my innocence! They stole my life! They stole my soul! They stole all hope of ever being free, as I was swapped back and forth for several years from my home to my aunt's.

Manipulating mind games were used. I was told that there would be no money for electricity, food, and milk for all the children if we did not do this.

At times, I could hear them talking about money as if my cousins and I were toys for sale.

I knew what we were doing was horribly wrong, and I hated it!

I just became a two-faced robot with no soul! "It" became routine, just like I automatically folded my blanket each morning without thinking, without feeling, and laid it aside.

My dark mask was worn at night. While at school, I would put on my pretend smile mask over my dark soul trying to survive another day until ... I ultimately lost myself. I let the darkness fill me, and I wanted to die.

I wrote a poem from the words that ran through my mind and heart over and over every night.

RESCUE ME
HELP ME!
Monsters are chasing!
Can't you see?
Monsters are whispering
Can't you hear?
Monsters are shouting—"You're nothing!"
Can't you feel my pain?
Monsters are pushing—"End it all—just jump!"
Can't you hear all the "Whys" I'm asking?
Monsters are laughing—"Ha-ha!
You're all alone in this darkness!"
CAN SOMEONE PLEASE RESCUE ME?

I am very thankful that God heard my cries and sent someone to rescue my sisters and cousins and me. However, at first, it was very scary because we thought most everyone were monsters and didn't believe that real love could ever exist for us.

When I first transitioned to the Village of Hope, I was convinced that if the Home Parents ever knew the secret dark side of Elly, I would be discarded; so, I wore my "Smile—I'm Ok, Elly Mask." However, day after day all the leaders at the Homes of Hope poured out

unconditional love on me. Eventually, I felt safe enough to slowly open up with Mom Kathleen, co-director of the homes. She told me that people around the world helped build the Homes at the Village of Hope to give children, just like me, a chance to find true love and hope.

Mom Kathleen told me part of her story and how God healed her heart from her own childhood pain. She said, "Now God is using my healed heart to help other children to know the God Who can heal the darkest and deepest past and give a brand-new life inside and out." She told me that God made sure someone heard my cries so I too could be rescued and healed. Most of all, she told me that God was the true Rescuer, Healer, and Lover of my soul.

It wasn't long until I was safely wrapped in Mom Kathleen's arms, sobbing, and all that was stuffed into the deepest, darkest closets of my soul poured out.

That glorious day, my incredible God came and rescued me from my sin, my anger, my shame, my pain, gave me a brand-new life and even a brand-new name. As God's Word and promises were poured into me, I began to embrace that I was no longer "Two-Faced Elly," unwanted and used as a pawn. I was now adopted as a daughter of the King and welcomed into the most loving family of God. That day, my name was changed to Elena, meaning "bright shining light."

I love my God and my new family at the Homes of Hope. I especially enjoy helping the new children adjust when they first enter the homes. Patiently, I love them where they are, so someday they too can take off their masks and feel safe enough to embrace the beautiful person God created them to be. Why? Because God's love, light, and life can dispel any darkness! In God's arms they really can be healed!

With a thankful heart,

God's Daughter and Bright, Shining Light,

— Elena

The light shines in the darkness, and the darkness has not overcome it. (John 1:5)

Heart Challenge

———

A fter reading Two-Faced Elly's story, you may be filled with questions, emotions, and hopefully also a righteous cry for justice. It should not take something happening directly to us to awaken our compassion to trigger an action.

Elena's words do shout a wake-up call and shine a bright light on the many more children still hidden in plain sight who need to be rescued, redeemed, and restored from this silent dark web epidemic. Wherever the dark is the darkest, that is where we at Compassionate Hope choose to run with the love and light of Christ.

Will you pick up your light and run with us?

May Elena's voice echo deep into each of our hearts!

PART 3

IT'S NOT OK!
GOTTA OWN IT TO WIN IT!

I (Al) and two of my young "Timothy disciples" were having breakfast with Mr. John, one of our big-hearted Compassionate Hope supporters. I say "big-hearted" not because of his giving but because of his sensitive, tender heart before God. I was giving him an update on what God was doing through Compassionate Hope Foundation (CHF) because of supporters like him and started sharing about our work in the Philippines with the OSEC children.

Before I could even finish explaining the acronym for OSEC (Online Sexually Exploited Children), we watched as Mr. John humbly began to weep. He tightly grabbed my son Isaac on the shoulder and gasping through his words, he said:

"We should NOT have an acronym for something like that. It is not all right! It is not OK!" Shaking his other fist in the air, he said: "I do not apologize for breaking down, but rather, I apologize to God for letting something like this happen on my watch. I live on this planet, and this is just not right!"

Mr. John humbly owned it, as should all of us!

As we got into the car, I looked into the red, tear-stained eyes of my two young Timothy disciples. They both sat in silence. I knew God was speaking volumes. Later that day, one young Timothy disciple, Corbin, wrote these words, and I dare say, they should be our own:

"Lord, I am so humbled by Mr. John's heart, by his tenderness, and his empathy. I sit here and think how selfish I am for having lived so long being 'OK' with something like this going on. Mr. John took this horrific sin going on in our world upon himself and was repenting for it. He began to speak as if everything going forward would be him doing whatever possible he could to not let it continue to happen.

"God, I cry from my heart, 'Lord, this is what I want my generation to experience: to feel Your heart, God, like Papa Al and Mr. John do.' And then immediately, I thought to myself, 'No Lord, please! I beg You to start with me! I beg You to make me break like this! I beg You to not let me ever be even remotely 'OK' knowing such things are going on in the world, but realize that I still have a larger part to play in this redemption. I beg You to come and humble me. I beg You to make my heart tender. I beg You to help me feel, see, and think more in the way that You do. I take this conviction upon my head for sitting here realizing how selfish my life has been, and how much I set my life up to be about 'me!' I've set so much of my life around relationships, being driven by fear of rejection, to be seen, valued, and acknowledged by people. Forgive me, for seeking credit out of fear and pride. I don't want to focus on my kingdom, even in the subtle ways I've been trained by my flesh to do. Thank You, Lord, for the opportunity to be a part of what You are doing to rescue, restore, redeem priceless children into Your kingdom. I'm humbled that You've led me to Yourself and how You led me to join You in Your work through Compassionate Hope Foundation to make a difference!

"Lord, give me more of a heart like I saw this morning. You are so unbelievably good to us! Thank You for allowing me to feel Your heart through Mr. John. Thank You for that experience and blessing me with it, Lord. Forgive me of my sin! I love You, Lord. I'm Your servant. Show me how I can make a difference!"

— *Corbin*

HOW SHOULD I RESPOND?

It takes people like Mr. John, Corbin, and each of us bearing a personal responsibility to "own it" before we can step up to begin to win this battle of injustice against our most precious treasure in the world—our children.

It takes people who say, "I still have a part to play in fighting for the redemption of children who can't fight for themselves."

It takes people pushing aside their hesitancy to open up their own hearts to feel the grieving, broken heart of the Father over the unimaginable, horrific pain of these precious children and say they are worth our moving to sacrificial action.

It takes people to understand the wonderful and fulfilling opportunity to join our Father in laying down our own selfish ways, our own lives, in order to watch and pray, and be moved in obedience to serve these rescued ones.

It takes people seeing the urgency of the epidemic and saying, "I will join with you in this fight, in this life-saving—life-giving—mission for those rescued from this dark web however I can."

It takes people's voices praying and crying out, "Enough is enough!" It takes people with skin on to run into the darkness and simply sit down beside a broken, hurting child till they can see a glimpse of His light of hope. Perhaps you can relate to once being that broken one feeling all alone.

What is the one thing needed to change an OSEC child's future?

That one thing is ... YOU and YOUR choice to rise up, stand up, speak up, and step in with intentional action.

Who will join Elly's voice for the voiceless? Who will fight to rescue and restore hope for the next Elly?

Who will take personal responsibility and stand up with us and say, "I will be that one to help reach that one still crying in the darkness!"

> But if anyone has the world's goods and sees his brother in need, yet closes his heart against him, how does God's love abide in him? Little children, let us not love in word or talk but in deed and in truth. (1 John 3:17–18)

Choose to BE THE ONE and together let's run into the darkness with HOPE!

**LEARN MORE ABOUT HOW YOU
CAN JOIN THE FIGHT WITH JUSTICE
AND HOPE AGAINST HUMAN TRAFFICKING
AND THE OSEC EPIDEMIC:**

www.CompassionateHope.org/philippines

**YOU CAN ALSO WATCH TIM AND
DEMI TEBOW WITH TIM TEBOW
FOUNDATION SHARE ELLY'S STORY**

www.CompassionateHope.org/timtebowfoundation

FINAL HEART CHALLENGE

We pray this journey through *Breaking Invisible Chains* challenges you to a bolder faith in a faithful, redeeming God. You might say that some stories were a "beautiful mess"—messy because of injustice and the depravity of man's greed and sin.

But the stories were also beautiful because you witnessed God's redemptive, sovereign hand reach in and remold what was broken into a marvelous masterpiece showcasing His glory! Christ bore scars on Calvary so that He could heal our scars. The reality is that Christ is our Rescuer Who came to rescue you and me from our human slavery of sin. We pray you can see clearly that your scars are beautiful, tangible reminders of what Christ has redeemed and made new. Perhaps now is the time to start your journey and embrace what you have been set free from and free to, then pass on to others the keys to unlock their invisible chains.

Several themes challenging us all to a courageous, contagious faith were woven into a beautiful veil wrapped around each person in this book.

— The stories of unbound, uncontainable faith remind us of the radical price persecuted believers are willing to pay for the Gospel to go forth to set people free. We pray that the bold faith of the grieving widow challenges you to use your voice and roar like a lion in prayer and to shut the lying mouth of the lurking enemy.

— The beauty of redemption that was woven into the transformed hearts of the abandoned, abused, and trafficked helps us believe by faith that if God did it for them, then He can bring healing in our own lives. Once we embrace the reality of being released from the invisible chains that bind us, we too can walk by faith in full liberty available in Christ.

— Woven into each story is the call to stand and fight for justice for those who can't fight for themselves. How do we start to become a battle-ready partner? Like Nehemiah, we start on our knees, repenting for our sin and that these atrocities happened on our watch. Then ask God, "How do I personally help engage in this battle of injustice?" This is God's work, and we are His instruments He has chosen to use. Are you ready? He awaits your enlistment.

WITH GRATEFUL HEARTS

Thank you for walking this journey with us. We hope you see a tiny glimpse of what we see, feel what we feel, and sense the joy of knowing that you are playing a role in seeing someone set free. Jesus came to set the captives free, and there is no joy like looking into the face of someone who knew bondage and now knows liberty for the first time.

When Susan and I surrendered to the Lord's call, it was simply a "Here we are Lord—send us." We never dreamed of the roads we would travel around the world, and in a blink of an eye, here we stand at the crossroad intersecting with you and sharing just a few of those life-impacting stories.

We kneel, praying that these freedom stories of hope will inspire you to courageous faith and shine a light to guide you in your heart journey of freedom and transforming hope. We pray that these stories have touched your heart in a way that will mobilize you to take action.

We pray you hear God's cry, "Help My suffering body," and embrace God's call to rise up and become a light in the darkness. Our light shines brighter together!

Your journey partners,

— *Al and Susan Henson*

Founders of Compassionate Hope Foundation

ACKNOWLEDGMENTS

Breaking Invisible Chains was written to testify to the redemptive power of the Gospel of grace and dedicated to our true Rescuer Jesus, Who sets captives free.

> A special thanks to the courageous charac-
> ters in these God stories, the servant-lead-
> ers of the Homes of Hope, and to those who
> collaborated to create this book for the sake
> of rescuing and restoring of the "least of
> these" in the Homes of Hope.

Words could never express the gratitude Susan and I feel for the many who have chosen to walk this journey of life with us. The God stories we have witnessed and lived out over the last forty-five years are limitless, and so is the love from the beautiful people we've embraced along the way.

First, we want to acknowledge the courageous characters in the true stories highlighted in this book. These are their God stories of rescue and redemption. We are honored that God allowed us to intersect with their stories to make them a tiny part of our story as well.

Second, we honor the beautiful lives of those first persecuted refugees who walked into our hearts at the front door of Lighthouse Ministries and to those early, invaluable servants who walked alongside them. The earnest heart plea and prayer of these redeemed refugees compelled us to embark with them on this lifelong mission of seeing the good news of the Gospel taken to their families in their homelands.

Thirdly, we want to acknowledge those early supporters who by faith believed in us, the mission, and the calling to rescue the "least of these" through establishing Homes of Hope through Compassionate Hope Foundation. Some opened doors of connection, purchased land, built buildings, and supported the homes and our CHF team servants. Other faithful supporters and amazing foundations have since become battle-ready partners—coming alongside extraordinary national leaders. Together with God, we are rescuing, restoring, and seeing thousands of redeemed hearts brought into Homes of Hope. Ministry is never an "I" but a "we," and these vulnerable, broken children would not know freedom without the "we." Each of you are invaluable and treasured gifts!

Finally, we want to acknowledge the many who have supported the mission of this book. We want to personally thank our CHF team and all those who helped through prayer, financial aid, editing, marketing, and focus groups. We are also thankful for all the encouragement from our incredible coaching/publishing team, HigherLife Publishing, who believed in the message and heart of this book.

A special thanks to all of you on this journey, all for the sake of those who still need to be rescued!

With grateful hearts,

— Al and Susan Henson

Download our free
Homes of Hope Booklet

HOMES OF HOPE

Rescuing "The Least of These" in Southeast Asia

COMPASSIONATE H PE

You've read their stories; now see where our children live, learn, love, heal, and grow.

www.CompassionateHope.org/home-of-hope-book

COMPASSIONATE
H⌂PE

Compassionate Hope is a Christ-centered global charitable organization focused on providing hope and a future to victims and potential victims of human trafficking and religious persecution in Southeast Asia, one future leader at a time.

Our 55+ Homes of Hope in Southeast Asia welcome these children into a loving, family environment where their physical, spiritual, emotional, educational, and vocational needs are met.

Will you help break the chains of poverty and abuse?

Donate Today

Invite Al & Susan to Your Event or Podcast

Al and Susan Henson are the founders of Compassionate Hope Foundation. They have spent more than forty years walking with the nations, discipling and mentoring leaders, and rescuing "the least of these."

Al and Susan welcome the opportunity to share what God is doing in Southeast Asia with your church, school, podcast, conference, or other events.

To inquire about their availability, contact connect@compassionatehope.org

If you have been encouraged by *Breaking Invisible Chains*, will you help us spread the word?

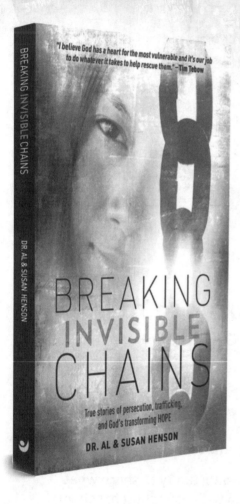

There are several ways you can help share about *Breaking Invisible Chains*:

- Recommend the book to your friends. Word-of-mouth is the best advertising!

- Leave a review on Amazon.

- Post about the book on your social media account.

- Blog about the book or share an excerpt with a link to CompassionateHope.org. You have our permission to share excerpts as long as you provide proper credit and a link.

- Purchase extra copies to give as gifts.

**Have ideas or questions for us?
Reach out to Al & Susan
at connect@compassionatehope.org**

www.CompassionateHope.org